Praise for *Th*

What a powerful book! Robert N. Ruesch and his daughter Jennifer have given us a wonderful gift of their heartfelt story of a life of addiction and deception. This father-daughter story is a passionate story of real life, hurt, pain, and victory. It is a must read for anyone who struggles with addiction of any kind. It is also for any parent who grieves the decisions of their children. This book is an honest, raw look at the demons of addiction and the love and support of a father. Your soul will be enriched as you journey with two amazing individuals.

Dr. Arnie Guin
Lead Pastor
Southwest Community Church-Littleton, CO.

Robert N. Ruesch hits a nerve that is American life in this generation. It is raw pain in ink and paper that strikes at the very heart of what so many families are experiencing.

He not only describes his daughter's descent into addiction, but he also speaks to what drove her there. This book is filled with sadness, brokenness, and heartache for sure. But this journey also has what every life hungers for . . . hope. There is hope, and Jennifer's story should give rise to that hope for every family on this heartbreaking journey.

Rev. Michael Gantt
MK Gantt Ministries
Brattleboro, Vermont

At a time of so many arguments and conflicts over how personal and social issues should be concluded with these intransigent problems, it is extremely important to read and encounter the real responses of our fellow travelers on earth. Responses made in the reality of experience make issues far more than just facts. Agreeing or disagreeing with how someone decides can and will happen but to not know someone's life and experience make conclusions hollow arguments. Here is an honest person giving you her life and experiences in real rough spots, and you would be a fool not to read and ponder.

Larry Yoder
Critical Reader, Developmental Editor

This is a story of hope being pushed aside, first by an abusive step-parent, then by alcohol and drug addiction. Multiple recovery programs are stymied by failure. Finally, recovery is assisted by a persistent parent, who is writing this book together with his daughter. They, by the grace of God, make this a story of hope restored.

Les Strobe
Writer & Editor

A unique contribution of this book is the story of healing for a person struggling with addiction and giving voice to those who are concerned significant others (CSOs). A key part of healing for each is to have a strong faith in God. This is a story of transformation seen at its best as told in first person. Transformation for both, one searching for recovery and CSOs, especially her parents. Those in treatment will benefit from reading and processing this book.

Dr. Jack Perkins, D.Min., LACD

The Long Road Home

A Family's Journey
Through Addiction

ROBERT N. RUESCH
WITH JENNIFER LYN RUESCH

ILLUMIFY
MEDIA.COM

The Long Road Home
Copyright © 2024 by Robert N. Ruesch

All rights reserved. No part of this book may be reproduced in any form or by any means—whether electronic, digital, mechanical, or otherwise—without permission in writing from the publisher, except by a reviewer, who may quote brief passages in a review.

All Scripture quotations (unless otherwise indicated) are taken from the Holy Bible, New International Version®, NIV®. Copyright © 1973, 1978, 1984, 2011 by Biblica Inc.™ Used by permission of Zondervan. All rights reserved worldwide. www.zondervan.com. The "NIV" And "New International Version" are trademarks registered in the United States Patent and Trademark office by Biblica, Inc.™

Scripture quotations marked (NKJV) are taken from the New King James Version®. Copyright © 1982 by Thomas Nelson. Used by permission. All rights reserved.

Disclaimer: The names used in this book are not the real names; they have been changed to protect identities.

The views and opinions expressed in this book are those of the author and do not necessarily reflect the official policy or position of Illumify Media Global.

Published by
Illumify Media Global
www.IllumifyMedia.com
"Let's bring your book to life!"

Paperback ISBN: 978-1-964251-22-6

Cover design by Debbie Lewis

Printed in the United States of America

Dedicated to anyone who has been on or is currently on a challenging journey away from alcohol or prescription drugs. And to the many caught in the web of deceit and lies, walking toward near death.

To the many family members who have cried silently or out loud as they watched the human train wreck, the person they love, travel down the tracks at neck-breaking speed, knowing and fearing what the result could be. To those living in fear that there will be a call or a notification or a police officer at your door asking to come in, telling you to sit down. You already know the possible fatal news.

This father-daughter book is dedicated to all of you and your journey. Remember, there is hope in the Lord. Trust Jesus, trust Jesus; we did.

When we come to the end of ourselves,
we come to the beginning of God.
—Billy Graham

Contents

Introduction ix
Timeline xiii
Chapter One: First Drink 1
Chapter Two: Pure Anger 9
Chapter Three: Negative Relationships 16
Chapter Four: I Have Multiple Sclerosis 24
Chapter Five: Lives Lost 31
Chapter Six: Another Crisis and Conflict 41
Chapter Seven: Teen Challenge 51
Chapter Eight: Going to Prison 59
Chapter Nine: Being in Prison 68
Chapter Ten: Psychological Diagnosis 75
Chapter Eleven: Re-offended 84
Chapter Twelve: The Addict and the Narcissist ... 93
Chapter Thirteen: Near Death 103
Chapter Fourteen: Rehabilitation in San Antonio ... 110
Chapter Fifteen: Going Home 118
Chapter Sixteen: Getting Out 126
Chapter Seventeen: The Future 134
Chapter Eighteen: Getting Help 142
A Drug User's Prayer 148
My Name Is Meth 149
The Author of Life 152
Conclusion 153
Acknowledgments 156
Notes 158
About the Authors 159

Introduction

Drugs: the scourge and scar on America. "According to the National Center for Drug Abuse Statistics (NCDAS), almost 32 million people (11.7 percent of the population) were actively using drugs as of 2021, with marijuana, prescription stimulants, and methamphetamine as the most popular drugs of choice."[1] According to The Sentencing Project, "Women in state prisons are more likely than men to be incarcerated for a drug or property offense. Twenty-five percent of women in prison have been convicted of a drug offense, compared to 12% of men in prison; 19% of incarcerated women have been convicted of a property crime, compared to 13% among incarcerated men."[2]

With cities creating "safe zones" for users, you can witness the horror of seeing friends or family members overdose, recover, and overdose again and yet again. Then, in more cases than anyone wants to accept, finally succumb to death. And you, as a parent, a friend, even a case worker, can do nothing about it. The feeling of helplessness overcomes you like a dark and angry cloud. So many times, friends and family members are gone forever. The drug has taken their life; it had already stolen their livelihood and their persona. If there is an epidemic in the United States, the use of illegal street drugs is definitely at or close to the top of the list. Overdoses, relapses, new "clients"—every day you hear about someone who is hooked, almost dead, or dead. New and more powerful drugs cross the border of the United States, hidden in cars, boxes, and people.

Fentanyl breaches the border like an angry tornado. People, unsuspecting individuals, take a drug laced with death, and the result of swallowing a simple, little, "innocent" pill is just that: death. Then the survivors must deal with the fatal loss. There are never enough tears.

When Jennifer was fourteen, she discovered and started using alcohol, drinking it to "dull the hurt," as she says. Why? Because a male stepparent started abusing her and told her to tell no one, especially her biological parents. At first, drinking was just a swallow or two, then three or four, and finally most of the bottle. She will tell you that vodka was her choice. She concealed her drinking, the bottle, and the abusive relationship as the sexual abuse persisted day in and day out.

The child who wanted to *dull the hurt* became a prisoner of the bottle. The pills would soon be on the menu just to get through the day, the night, and the weekend. Never, never tell, keep it a secret, just endure, and try to get by. Become an alcoholic zombie. Grades would fall from high scores to failing marks with each burning swallow of booze. But, hey, the hurt was dulled, and that counted until it didn't matter what the reason was, just to swallow and to be swallowed up by a fog-shrouded world of nothingness.

Friends were not a priority. A bottle of booze became the top priority. Social activities, sure, but only with people who could get the needed booze, drug, or fix. And keeping the secret that was slowly killing this innocent child was a close second.

This is a story of tragedy to hope. Recovery from alcohol and drugs, recovery from being a continual victim to becoming a survivor. A victory of life over addiction, over impending death. This is also a story about a father's feeling

Introduction

of helplessness at seeing his daughter careening down a path of certain self-destruction and trying everything to stop the usually inevitable ending. A story of the void of not being able to rescue a precious daughter, a life created in the image of God being manipulated and impaled by Satan.

This battle has lasted over forty years, with continual attempts at rehab only to see Jennifer relapse again and again. A herculean fight for the very life and soul of a child. Jennifer is now a mature woman who has so much to give to society and a deep love to help others but, up until now, not herself.

In the next chapters, you will read of the defeats, brushes with death, and rescues, only to see a loved one fall back into the clutches of addiction again and again. And finally, not a complete victory, but a win on the side of recovery. The battle goes on each day, with each heartbeat. Satan does not rest; however, neither does Jesus.

Timeline

July 1, 1974	Jennifer was born in Denver, CO, and lived at Snow Mountain Ranch in Granby, CO.
April 1, 1979	Mother left family to work as a police officer in the Denver Metro area.
July 1979	Father divorced Mother. Jennifer was living with Father.
Oct. 1981	Father remarried. Verbal abuse from Stepmom started.
Oct. 1982	Moved to Loma Mar, CA. Father worked at Alameda County YMCA.
Sept. 1983	Father divorced (again).
Nov. 84–85	Father worked at San Jose Ambulance. Jen lived with Dad during that year.
Aug. 1988	Jen moved in with Mother. Abuse by Stepdad began. Started drinking; became an alcoholic.
Dec. 85–Oct. 88	Father worked for a Christian housing company. Jen lived with Dad for one year. Went to a public school in Oakland, CA.
Nov. 88	Father moved back to CO and married his high school sweetheart.
June 1992	Jen graduated from high school.

Sept. 1992	Attended Metro State College; quit mid-semester.
Sept. 1992	Started work at Perkins Restaurant.
March 1993	First pregnancy (19 years old); resulted in abortion in March.
April 1993	Met Paul, a known drug dealer.
May 1993	Mother graduated from law school and was hired by a prestigious law firm that defends police officers. Jennifer's first arrest for possession of marijuana; not charged.
March 1994	Found out Paul was cheating on Jennifer.
May 1994	Stepdad charged and arrested and trial date set for abuse of a child in a position of trust began.
June 1994	Mother quit the law firm; moved to the Bahamas.
July 1994	Jennifer moved in with boyfriend Paul.
Aug. 1994	Stepdad trial started. Accused on three counts for child molestation.
Sept. 1995	Stepfather found guilty of child abuse. Jennifer testified in court; Mother didn't come back from the Bahamas to support or testify.
Oct. 1997	Jennifer went to Florida, then lived with Mother in the Bahamas for a month.
Nov. 1997	Came back to Florida from the Bahamas and moved in with a married couple. Met Matt at a nightclub.

Timeline

Dec. 1997	Became pregnant from Matt on the first date, resulting in an abortion.
March 1998	Lived with Matt in Florida.
Oct. 1998	Grandmother flew Jennifer to Colorado to see her and Dad.
Oct. 1998	Miscarriage number one.
Dec. 19, 1999	Gave birth to son Kaleb in Florida.
April 2000	Moved back to Colorado with son Kaleb and husband Matt.
Oct. 2000	Enrolled in Concord Career Institute; received diploma as medical assistant. Worked in a medical office for one year.
Sept. 2001	Diagnosed with multiple sclerosis.
Sept. 2004	Moved back to Ft. Lauderdale, FL.
June 2006	Entered rehab at Wayside for Women for six months.
July 2006	Matt asked for divorce.
Oct. 2007	Jennifer had to take her cat of ten years to the animal shelter along with son's cat, as Matt delivered them to rehab.
Oct. 2009	Moved in with Father because a drug dealer threatened Jen's life.
Feb. 2010	Admitted to Teen Challenge in Midland, TX; stayed in the program fifteen months.
May 2011	Jen had a private room on Teen Challenge campus. Was asked to leave because of involvement with a male TC student, which was not allowed.

June 2011	Moved into an apartment in Midland; reconnected with the drug community.
May 2011– Jan. 2013	Worked at FedEx; fired for stealing.
Feb. 2013– July 2013	Worked at Hobby Lobby; let go because of not showing up for shifts, per company policy.
July 2013– Oct. 2013	Employed at T.J. Max. Quit job because of relationship with another person, which became an abusive relationship.
Nov. 2013	Arrested on federal drug charge.
March 2014	Released on bond. Went back to apartment in Midland for three months.
July 2014	Self-surrendered to federal prison. Sentenced with aiding and abetting, with possession of over 5 grams of methamphetamine and intent to distribute. Sentenced to thirty-six months with five years' probation.
April 2016	Released from federal prison. Went back to Midland, Texas.
Nov. 2016	Violated probation; went back to federal prison for six months.
May 2017	Released to Teen Challenge, waiting for rehab assignment.
July 2017	Assigned and admitted to Alpha Home in San Antonio.
Oct. 2017	Employed at discount store; became assistant manager.

Timeline

March 2018	Hospitalized for seizures.
June 2018	Hospitalized for overdose of gabapentin (Neurontin).
July 2018	Fired from the discount store because of drug usage (huffing).
Aug. 2018	Moved in with Minus One.
Dec. 2018	Admitted to SAT Behavioral Health Center for one week.
Dec. 2021	Received final Decree of Divorce from Matt, a twenty-year procedure.
March 9, 2022	Overdosed on meth/fentanyl; stopped breathing but was revived.
March 2022	Admitted to San Antonio Recovery for a month of rehab.
April 2022	Moved back to Evergreen with Father and Stepmom.
June 2022	Went back to Minus One; sent a text message to Father, saying she was staying in San Antonio.
Sept. 2023	Relationship with Minus One became more violent.
Oct. 2023	Moved back (again) with Father and Stepmom. Recovering, learning to love self.
Nov. 2023	Last name changed to Ruesch, creating personal self-identity.

Chapter One

First Drink

"To Numb the Hurt"

But seek first his kingdom and his righteousness, and all these things will be given to you as well.
—Matthew 6:33

Jennifer's Story

I started drinking at fourteen. It was an easy choice and, for me, the only choice, but not because of peer pressure. I needed to dull the hurt of my stepfather overstepping my personal physical bounds. I will explain, but first, I want to share some of my personal history.

I was born on my grandfather's birthday, July 1st. He and I always had a special relationship. I guess being born on his birthday was as special to him as it is to me, as is the fact that we were both left-handed.

My mom left me when I was in kindergarten to become a police officer. She broke through the glass ceiling of the police department she worked for. I am proud of her. But being abandoned at six years old broke my heart. I could not understand why she just up and left. I didn't know what I did wrong, but I knew in my heart that she left because of something I did. And I didn't know how to solve it and bring my mom back. Now I see it was not about me, nor was it my fault. I so wanted her love. I wanted to hear her voice and have her wake me up in the morning and kiss me goodnight. But she was gone. One day she was here, the next day, she had disappeared like smoke in the wind.

Nothing my dad could do seemed to repair the emotional trauma I felt from being abandoned by a maternal parent. Again and again, I asked myself, *Was it me that caused her to leave? What did I do? Can I get her back? Can we be a family again, like we were? Can you tell me why, why did she leave?* My father continued to say it had nothing to do with me, but I was not sure. All I knew was, I needed a mom, and a mom was not there.

Among all the days, there was one that was the hardest for me. I could not stop crying. That day at school, I was in trouble most of the day. I was hurt and angry, and I acted out, striking out at everyone and everything.

I know Dad got a call from the school. Daddy always picked me up at the highway, which was a mile from our home. As I got in the vehicle, I slammed my lunch pail and backpack down. Nothing was said until we arrived home.

Usually, Daddy would check in at the resort where he worked. Today we went directly home. He sat me down on the butcher-block table in our kitchen. I remember him looking into my eyes with an intensity I had not seen. And he promised he would always be there for me and would never leave me. It sounded good, but, as far as I was concerned, I didn't know. One parent had left. Could you tell me why the other parent would not depart to places unknown? Mom had told me she would always be my mom, but she was gone. How can you be a mom when you are gone? Would Daddy

First Drink

do the same thing, and then where would I go and who would I live with? I feared I would come home and find that Daddy had gone just like Mom had.

Daddy stayed with me. Our relationship, although sometimes rocky, was and is wonderfully special. His promise of never leaving me has always been fulfilled. Even when we did not live together, we have had the special bond that a daughter craves from her dad.

From first grade through third grade, I lived with my father. In fourth grade, I wanted to know who my mom was, and my father agreed to a year of living with her. She was seldom home; being a police officer, her shifts were never family friendly. I became a latchkey kid. I woke up on my own, went to school, and often came home to an empty house, which was better than being in the house with my stepfather. More of that trauma later.

In the fifth and seventh grades, I lived with my daddy, and in the sixth grade, I lived with my mom. In eighth grade I lived with my mom and her now police officer husband. That was when things started to unravel.

Like a ball of yarn tossed into the wind, my life became a whirlwind of intrusion, secrets, veiled threats, and ever increasing self-doubt. Can you tell me why a person would do what my stepdad thought was normal, do what he would do? I didn't invite any of the few friends over to my house (it was *not* a home) because I didn't know what awaited me behind the doors of the house. Well, I knew, and that was my secret. I believe this was the beginning of me burying my thoughts and not sharing with anyone. I would simply agree, perhaps say, "I know," and move on.

Even though I was "living" with my mom, she was never home. Her police work was comprised of classes, extra shifts, and who knows what. However, my stepdad was home. He worked a separate shift from my mom in the same police department. He and I were alone in the house more than I wanted. I was always afraid of him, even in the rare cases when we were all home together.

You keep secrets; you bury the invasive hurt deep in your soul. You try to protect who you are by becoming completely void of feelings. You live by one emotion, and that is anxiety: fear of what is going to happen when you are home alone and there is not another adult to protect you from prying hands and eyes.

I believe God defends your identity by securing your personality in a sanctuary evil cannot infiltrate. You become a living shell, not the vibrant person God intended you to be. You have His protection, yet you are vulnerable to the assault of evil. I don't know what hell is like, but I have seen physical, sexual evil on earth, and if that is a window into the way eternal hell is, I am thankful I have accepted Christ as my Savior.

Psalm 23 is a psalm I wish I would have known and memorized in the traumatic years of middle school and high school:

> *The Lord is my shepherd, I lack nothing.*
> *He makes me lie down in green pastures,*
> *he leads me beside quiet waters,*
> *he refreshes my soul.*
> *He guides me along the right paths*
> *for his name's sake.*
> *Even though I walk*
> *through the darkest valley,*
> *I will fear no evil,*
> *for you are with me;*
> *your rod and your staff,*
> *they comfort me.*

First Drink

*You prepare a table before me
in the presence of my enemies.
You anoint my head with oil;
my cup overflows.
Surely your goodness and love will follow me
all the days of my life,
and I will dwell in the house of the Lord
forever.*

We didn't go to church except perhaps on Christmas and Easter, if then. I don't know if my mom is a Christian; I pray she is. I would like to bring her to Christ, or back to Christ. What I know is, living in a lie is pure, intense hell on earth. Keeping secrets because of threats is incorrect. You learn as you live life experiences, and what you do with this knowledge is up to you. Not sharing continues the lie. So the scab of life comes off. And I hope and pray that sharing about the life I have not lived for Christ and the addiction I continue to battle will help others have the courage to confront the dragon and slay evil with truth.

A Father's Response

You were thought to be a premature baby, but after talking to the doctor, the medical team decided you were born as a full-term baby. You were a mountain baby, developed at over 8,000 feet above sea level. And you were born in Denver, not in the high country, as there was not a birthing center for you to come into this world where we lived.

You were not breathing when you were delivered, and that was when the medical rodeo started. Hearing the doctor say, "We will try one more time to get her to breathe," my heart broke for you trying to fight for your new life. I cried out with urgent prayers to God for you to live, to be a part of our family. To be my daughter.

The doctor and the nurses were working overtime to get you to breathe. Blue was not a color I wanted to see on you, and you were turning more and more a darker shade of blue every second. Then, with a new baby sound that could have broken glass, you took your first breath, turned a beautiful living pink, and were mad as all get-out. Wailing, tossing your arms and legs about, and ready to take on the world just as soon as you calmed down. You became a living, breathing, screaming soul, fighting for each breath. Concern from the medical team turned into smiles. Your breathing on your own replaced the stress of the situation with comfortable, confident relief. You were alive! A new child, formed by God, entered the world.

I followed my tears of fear with tears of unbridled joy. I had a baby daughter. Your name would be Jennifer Lyn Ruesch, and you would take on the world and change the world. A merciful and loving God had answered the urgent prayers for you to live. This beautiful baby girl would be one of His children.

However, your battle for life was far from over. The next three and a half decades would show that. Soon after you were born, the doctor diagnosed you with jaundice, and you were in an incubator for several days.

During the incubator days, we could only hold you for a short amount of time. The rest of the time was a lonely, sterile, warm, and, I would imagine, scary time for you. So new to the world and so far away from the loving touch of parents. Encased in a plastic cocoon, your welcome to the world was as sterile as it could be. Yet the medical criteria allowed you to live, established you as a survivor from day one.

First Drink

For the next few years, a new mother and father cuddled, loved, cherished, and nourished you. We took care of every need you had. Life was safe and simple. Feed you, change your diapers, let you sleep, repeat. Some friends came to our home when the hospital discharged you. When they walked in, they said, "It smells like a new baby here." I had not thought of that, but the house had a new resident, a new life. I was a proud papa. You became the focused light of my world.

Fast-forward to kindergarten when your mom left. And that was when the trauma of parental abandonment set in. I saw the hurt in your eyes. Part of your sparkle was hidden or gone, or maybe buried deep in your innocent soul. I know you felt the breakup was your fault, your doing. Your thought was, if only you could have been better, nicer, happier, then maybe your mom would have stayed.

Your mom leaving was not remotely your doing or fault. Sometimes issues beyond anyone's control can enter and cause division. Bottom line was that a mom left her marriage and child. The dissolution of our marriage was never your fault. If there was anyone who was culpable, it was me, your father. And those were my issues.

Finding out now about the abuse from your stepdad, the secret you have kept buried for decades, breaks my heart. No one, not you or anyone else, should have to go through such a devastating trauma. (Dads should know or suspect when there is something not right in their children's lives. I would defend the safety of my child, defend to death.) You experienced the death of your childhood, when things should have been a safe, happy, carefree time.

A fit of righteous anger spills out from my soul, along with a deep sorrow, knowing you did not receive any protection from the evil imposed upon you. It took your mom's divorce from this evil person, and discovery by the authorities, to stop the abuse, but for you and several others, the damage was done. (We now know repairs were years in the future. Therapy couldn't numb the hurt when you kept secrets out of fear, which led to your downward spiral. Down into a pit of anger, helplessness, and negative self-worth.)

Yet I continue to see in you a fighter, someone who wishes to survive and succeed. As we, father and daughter, write this story of addiction, conviction, happiness, sorrow, and recovery, I hope we can find a resolution for each of us, and I hope to show others God's commitment and unconditional love. His absolute protection, His grace, His mercy. Your journey is now becoming an open book, perhaps a way, a path, for others to be helped out of their miry pit of despair to find everlasting hope.

Alone we can do so little; together we can do so much.
—Helen Keller

Chapter Two

PURE ANGER

*Refrain from anger and turn from wrath;
do not fret—it leads only to evil.
—Psalm 37:8*

Nothing like what happened to me should happen to anyone, boy or girl, man or woman. Yet we live in a fallen, sin-filled world. And yet here we are. Was I mad at the world and my circumstance? You bet I was, in some ways, still am. Every day, I work to deal with my anger, mostly hidden, and confront the anger.

This process of healing is hard but necessary if you want to heal and become the person God intended you to be. You must work on your recovery every moment of the day, lest the evil one finds an opening to worm his way back into your life.

You do not get over having a mom leave you (more than once), abuse by a stepdad, or getting physically beaten by multiple boyfriends. (Yes, I have a bad boy picker.)

Angry, feeling righteous indignation, and mad at the world. Feeling cheated, knowing full well the world was against me, you get it, that was me. When did I not hurt or get angry? Playing the victim's card was something I excelled at. I learned how to manipulate, convince, and tell partial truths to my advantage. I could get my way because I knew how to use my anger to my benefit until my luck ran out. That was

OK because I knew, without a doubt, I would replace luck with something disappointing, and that would allow me to get angrier. I mean, why not happiness? If I couldn't have it, I made darn sure others didn't have it either. I could do that, and I would do anything I could to survive. Get the picture? I, myself, only me. People have stepped on me and taken advantage of me. They could steal from me because I allowed it all my life. I believed that was my lifestyle. Doormat Jennifer. Welcome to my addictive world.

My daddy said more times than I can count, "I don't recall seeing a doormat with your name on it." Well, let me tell you, the doormat was there, and my boyfriends, friends, and strangers all wiped their emotionally filthy feet on it every day. And I let them!

However, in all the emotional madness I allowed myself to experience, there was always God's protection upon me. I didn't know it at the time. My guardian angels have many feathers missing from protecting me, that I know. I am a chosen one of God's children. "But you are a chosen people, a royal priesthood, a holy nation, God's special possession, that you may declare the praises of him who called you out of darkness into his wonderful light" (1 Peter 2:9). It has taken me many years to know and accept this in my heart.

Good choices, bad choices, worse choices, everything is now on the table, like lines of cocaine on the furniture. If you can sniff and swallow, if it makes you "happy" for a few brief moments, and if you are not angry, well, go for it. Better living through street drugs: that is what "they" say. Don't believe that for a heartbeat if you want to have a heartbeat. Drugs, any drugs, prescription, street, or stolen will eventually kill you. If you are lucky, you will survive, but with consequences. I lost all my teeth because of the drugs I craved. I lost my dignity, personal self-worth, and a willingness to live a positive life because of drugs. Drugs I found, stole, and "borrowed," given and dared to try, including huffing aerosol cans—you name it, I did it.

Imagine the sorrow God went through (and is sometimes still going through along with us) watching my free will being abused. Yet God was beside me. He continues to be my protector, guidance counselor, eternal friend. What a wonderful blessing to know He was and continues to be by my side. Even as this book is being written, His hand is on the sentences, the thoughts. He is writing the book. My dad and I are just placing the words on the page, directed by His eternal hand.

Here is how my life went. I was living in Florida, drinking, drugging, and "living the life." I was losing control and custody of my young son. My husband threatened multiple times to kick me out because I abused alcohol (and other things). Vodka was my choice of booze. It didn't show up on my breath, but it did in my behavior. Finally, he had enough, and out I went to my first rehab program at Wayside House, which I knew I did not need. This was a twelve-week-minimum program. The reason I agreed to go was to return to my child and "loving" husband. That didn't quite work out the way I planned. My husband informed me on his first visit that he was filing for divorce. Welcome to the shocking reality. I expected support and instead heard I was being kicked out of my family.

So, after multiple hospital visits, detox places, and continual discovery of my hidden booze (and I was good at hiding it), my husband had enough. Child protective services were called. They came, saw the disarray of our "home" and said we had twenty-four hours to clean up the apartment. If not, they would take our child and place him in foster care. Social services carted me off to another detox center. And my son's father stayed up for twenty-four hours cleaning and disinfecting our apartment. Throwing my vodka bottles out, trashing my drugs. And with that, I was a person without a family—no husband, no child. Just me and where my next fix and/or drink would come from.

My stuff was packed up and stored. He, the loving, supportive husband, made me give the cat I had loved for over a decade to an animal shelter. I never saw Madolyn again. Not even a goodbye. Just a statement. The cat was not part of the family, like me. Anger, you bet. Sorrow, yes. Feeling like a failure. I am sure the evil one was happy with the way my life was cascading down.

After rehab, I was not welcome or allowed (according to my estranged husband) to live with them. Not that I don't blame them. I was a drugged mess.

Two halfway houses later, I found an apartment, a cute little bungalow, and I started over for the first time of many. Some of my grandmother's favorite things were among the possessions I had. My job was in a restaurant on the wait staff. This was my usual and always fallback form of income. The stable of my life, a free meal with a working shift and a place to hook up with a street dealer. (After all, they need to eat and meet clients.) I met a drug dealer. I was told he could kill me. That did it. I called my dad to come and rescue me. Back to Colorado again.

Fast-forward: I was living with my dad and his wife back in Colorado. That lasted only a few months. They kicked me out as an adult because of using "legal" drugs. I called around and tried to find a place with friends. Ha, that didn't work. My friends knew my addiction and would not be a part of what I was doing.

You make choices, and choices come with either positive or negative consequences. My choices resulted in many more negative than positive situations. And that was what I believed my life would be. A continuing set of failures. Addiction does that to you. And you become addicted to failure. Not succeeding becomes your lifestyle. Success and positive experiences are foreign to you.

Welcome to my world.

Dad came down to Florida during this time to see me when I was working once. I hid my addiction well; he suspected nothing. I was fantastic at that. (Addiction and anger can give you skills you didn't realize you had.)

He even turned around on his trip home and gave me some extra cash before he drove off. Score one for more in the life of a person addicted to drugs! He really had no clue, and that made me mad. I wanted him to come and rescue me, save me from the tortured life I was living. Deep down, I wanted to be healed and live a loving life with my husband (whom I felt I really loved) and my son (whom I loved beyond measure and would do anything for.) Yet I could not reach out or cry out for help. Addiction makes you mentally and emotionally mute. You don't have a voice.

Drugs do the silent talking. They suck you down into a pit that you cannot get out of on your own. Yet you don't call out for help. Why? Because you firmly believe you can beat this drug or alcohol monkey that is on your back. You can beat addiction yourself. After all, you got you there, so you can reasonably get out of the clutch and claws of addiction. NOT A CHANCE without interceding rehabilitation help that you accept. That simple fact is hidden from you because of the addiction. Deep down you know you need help but don't seek it, and that makes you angry, more angry than you can handle. (Where did I hide my bottle? Who can I call to hook me up?) Like that will help. "He will cover you with his feathers, and under his wings you will find refuge; his faithfulness will be your shield and rampart" (Psalm 91:4). If I would have known that verse, believed it, and lived knowing God was there for me, things would have been better, but that is a rear-window view.

Anger is like an emotional cancer. Until you forgive yourself, you cannot move forward, and each day, each hour, your negative emotions rule the day. I remember reaching over as a passenger in the car and honking the horn because another driver had caught my wrath. Where did that come from? I believe you know.

Each day, I was mad about something. It didn't matter what. All I needed was a reason. I didn't even know what happiness was unless I was taking or swallowing something, and that was a false happiness.

I remember there was a day when I was so mad I was pounding on the window of my car. I wanted to break the window. Dad was watching me. I could not see the hurt in him. But I felt it when he said he was leaving to go home, and I needed to quit pounding on the car window. I didn't see him leave, as I was striking out about who knows what. It was and is what I did.

If there was any success or a positive relationship in my life, I worked to sabotage it, which made me more angry and want to do something, take anything, steal to make up for the hurt I was causing myself and others. I was and am an expert in the process of self-destruction.

OK, that is the negative, sorrow-filled life of a person not trusting God in their life. So many people are on a self-destructive path and never seem to get away from the addiction they have chosen. My heart now goes out to them because there is hope, there is always hope, even when the addict does not believe it or see it. We have a loving God who yearns for us to be in His loving will. When we realize His compassionate love for us and accept Him as our Savior, great and wonderful things will happen in our lives.

I am not saying being a Christian will make your life easy, but once you are, you have a fully undeniable, reliable source of strength, guidance, love, and commitment. You have an eternal team on your side. I wish I would have realized this many years before; however, I do now and that counts.

In the following chapters I describe times in my life when God was protecting me and keeping me in the safety of His hand. We have a magnificent Creator; we are made in His image. "So God created mankind in his own image, in the image of God he created them; male and female he created them" (Genesis 1:27). That says a lot, but then, in 2 Corinthians, we read the continuation of His glory in us. "And we all, who with unveiled faces contemplate the Lord's glory, are being transformed into his image with ever-increasing glory, which comes from the Lord, who is the Spirit" (2 Corinthians 3:18).

God's love is like an ocean.
You can see its beginning, but not its end.
—Rick Warren

Chapter Three

NEGATIVE RELATIONSHIPS

Do not be yoked together with unbelievers. For what do righteousness and wickedness have in common? Or what fellowship can light have with darkness?
—*2 Corinthians 6:14*

Let's face it: I have a bad picker when it comes to relationships with men and some women. Somehow, I focus on finding people who will hurt and walk all over me, even though many of my relationships started off on a positive note. "Doormat Jennifer" is not a moniker I like for myself, but it is the image I carried. Trying to change is difficult for a person who lives a life of addiction.

Let's dive into the challenge of change and uncover the truth about living a life tied to alcohol, drugs, and dead-end relationships.

Paul was my first love. He was also my weed dealer. I would find people who needed something, and I would be the middleman. This was a way I believed I could continue to prove my love for him. I thought he hung the moon. I would do anything for him, and he asked for everything. If he needed money, I was the bank. When he needed physical contact, I was the booty call, and I was on his speed dial. If it wasn't my stepdad strutting around in the buff, then it was Paul wanting to get—well, you know. My lifestyle was not

Negative Relationships

what I thought it should be; I had dreamed, like every little girl, of being a princess and having my prince. A prince in shining armor, riding up on a white horse. What I know now is that when you are in a negative relationship, you are the one to polish the armor. You are the one to clean up after the white horse, including everything else in the stables. I don't play the lottery—reference my bad picker—because I feel I will not choose the winning numbers.

This was my world of choosing people who were more than willing to take. Take advantage of me. My dad always said I would give my winter coat to a person who was freezing to keep them warm. That is a positive quality *if* you have boundaries.

I was being like everyone else, just not me. Making others happy, while I, myself, was frustrated and sad. Visual and emotional abuse entered my life as a child, with no parental awareness and the stepparent privy to my secret drinking. He strutted; I drank and pursued negative relationships. He was running around me in the buff, and I was involved in relationships that were not to my advantage.

Here is a recipe for a "friendship" that is not positive. All you need to do is add alcohol, drugs, and low self-esteem. Pour in a lot of victim poor-me phrases, stir in illegal opportunities to drink, do drugs, and smoke, and add a broken heart for good measure. Simmer with your life, bring to a boil, and you are hooked. I was a gourmet cook at boiling my life away.

Your emotional toll and physical stress will continue to lower your self-esteem. You become a doormat for every increasingly negative and nonproductive relationship you can imagine. These interactions with your "special one" will keep pushing you into a deeper emotional and physical pit. Only our Lord and Savior can save you from that trap. "If you declare with your mouth, 'Jesus is Lord,' and believe in your heart that God raised him from the dead, you will be saved. For it is with your heart that you believe and are justified, and it is with your mouth that you profess your faith and are saved" (Romans 10:9–10).

In the realm of mental health, negative relationships often serve as a breeding ground for toxic behaviors and coping mechanisms. People rely on unhealthy habits like substance abuse to numb the emotional pain linked to these relationships. Also, the constant stress and emotional turmoil can mess up sleep patterns, making mental health problems even worse. In my case, the stress would cause my MS to flare up. And then the drinking and drug use would increase. More flare-ups caused more alcohol abuse.

I would stay away from family functions because I believed I was not worthy, was not wanted, or could not contribute any positive energy to an event.

Negative relationships can also hinder personal and professional growth. Being negative and critical of yourself can chip away at your confidence, making it difficult for you to pursue goals or speak up in different areas of life. I know this causes missed opportunities, unfulfilled potential, and a sense of stagnation. All the criteria the evil one needs to destroy your life and strip the knowledge of who you are in God's eyes.

During high school, I avoided my dad's family gatherings even more. I always had an excuse why I could not attend a family function. Every Thanksgiving, my uncle would host a family gathering with all the excellent food you could eat. I think I went once. I missed out on the loving support of an extended family who could only love me from a distance. Those moments are gone forever, but the future moments are held by God, and I am looking forward to being a part of a family. Actually, I am now! What a blessing family can be!

Negative Relationships

Here is how important family can be. Jesus's first miracle was at a wedding, a family gathering. To me, that says that family was a focus of His ministry. I know broken families have more challenges than traditional families. I know that too well.

When you are spiraling down, many times you are doing this at warp speed. Here are some examples of when I sought and developed negative relationships.

In Teen Challenge (2010), I developed a friendship with one resident. I will call her Dusty. Dusty was as out of control as I was. We were to become two peas in a pod. We both got kicked out of Teen Challenge for drugs, breaking curfew, and having boyfriends, all of which were against the rules.

I rented an apartment, and Dusty became a connection, supplier, "friend," and go-to person for any drug I needed or thought I needed. She also knew other male and female suppliers, and the drug addiction ramped up. Dusty's guys were always around at my place. Drugs flowed like honey from a jar. She was well connected, and I got plugged into the circle of her nefarious drug addicts. I was once again hooked.

One guy asked if I had ever shot up meth. I said, "Nope, but I want to." Being the "gentlemen" that he was, he asked again, and I answered in the affirmative. That was the only time I shot up. I could have died. I believe if I had dosed a second time, I would have overdosed.

Guys moved in and out, without my permission more times than I want to admit. I would come home from work and there *he* would be. I paid the rent, bought the drugs, supplied the alcohol. He did nothing. I was "drug central," a patsy because of my desire to have a meaningful relationship. Dusty was there to help move illegal things along.

However, here is a spoiler alert. She got clean and now has a loving husband and an online company. Blessed things happen. We are in contact almost every day now, keeping each other accountable and sharing daily success stories. Loving ourselves. There is always hope, always a way out, and drugs are NEVER that way. Learn from Dusty and me.

Before we became clean, we would do anything for a fix. What happens when you make stupid choices and get arrested? That is in another chapter: "Going to Prison." Suffice to say, do stupid things, expect stupid consequences. My choices of friends reflected the self-image I had of who I was. I believed, because of the mental and emotional abuse of my stepdad, I was not worthy of anything that could be positive in my life. That is again the evil one's way of worming his way into your life. Taking you down one negative relationship at a time.

At some point, you are in the gutter of life. Everything you have drunk, swallowed, sniffed, shot up isn't working. That is the precise time Jesus can work with you and redeem you to a loving, productive life.

Dusty and I parted ways. Well, that is not exactly true. I regressed and went back to Minus One. (This person, Minus One, was my narcissistic boyfriend for six years.) She was so thankful I had gotten away from him, so when I was love bombed back by Minus One, that decision resulted in Dusty ending our friendship. Looking back, I can see where Dusty was holding me accountable. Losing her friendship hurt me deeply. When there is manipulation in a relationship, you are emotionally blinded.

Here is the blessing. As you will see in the following chapters, my eyes were finally opened wide. And Dusty and I rekindled our friendship. She was clean, free of drugs, and married with a beautiful child. We text back and forth and share our joy, our challenges, and our sorrows. As with Jesus, past issues are, or can be, forgiven. We are both stronger now. I can see where Dusty had to step away from the negativity of my decisions. I had to find out for myself that my consistent choices, my wrong choices of relationships, caused me to fail. Praise Jesus for His love for me. I am learning to love myself each day.

Recovery takes time. Negative habits are tough to break. My dad has said to me so many times, "When you quit hitting yourself in the head with a hammer, it is exciting how much better you will feel." I didn't understand that statement for most of my life. There wasn't a hammer in my case; I had a mallet. With this mallet, I was striking myself all the time.

As I look back on, let's say, at least fifteen negative relationships and the harm I did to myself and others, I am so thankful for family and friends. People who continued to believe in me when I didn't believe in who I was. *Was* being the key word here. As we know, Ephesians says, "Finally, be strong in the Lord and in his mighty power. Put on the full armor of God, so that you can take your stand against the devil's schemes. For our struggle is not against flesh and blood, but against the rulers, against the authorities, against the powers of this dark world and against the spiritual forces of evil in the heavenly realms" (Ephesians 6:10–12). The passage tells you what you need to defeat the powers of "this dark world": the full armor of God.

Listen to Paul's words: "Stand firm then, with the belt of truth buckled around your waist, with the breastplate of righteousness in place, and with your feet fitted with the readiness that comes from the gospel of peace. In addition to all this, take up the shield of faith, with which you can extinguish all the flaming arrows of the evil one. Take the helmet of salvation and the sword of the Spirit, which is the word of God" (Ephesians 6:14–17). Unpacking that passage is so simple and obvious. All the armor is in the defensive posture. You are not looking behind, but forward. The sword is your offense.

Could God's direction not be more obvious? Why, oh why, didn't I see this truth before? That answer is straightforward: the evil one blinds you and binds you to a dark will of his doing. Yet breaking the chains of darkness is so incredibly simple. Tell the evil one to get behind you, ask Jesus to be your Savior, and then your eternal journey starts.

I have a deep sorrow for all the negative people who were a part of my life for decades. My prayers are that they will see the eternal light of Jesus. My fear is that many of them have not seen His light but His wrath in their death because of drugs and violence. Each soul lost is lost forever. How much responsibility do I bear? Yet I know I am forgiven. I have accepted Jesus's salvation. What a joy that has brought to my life. Now the scales of blindness are being lifted every day.

A new dawning is happening. I realize I don't need so many vices in my life. I am satisfied with what the Lord is providing me. What a continued relief to see the positive side of living. I am not looking over my shoulder, wondering who I need to pay off for drugs or if someone is going to take more from me than I can give. I can see there are individuals I can trust: Christian friends who will come alongside me when I am weak or down.

My prayer is that as I grow away from all the minus things in my life, I can be a support for others who are going through what I went through. I looked for love in extremely wrong places. Drug dealers cannot offer lasting relationships. They are only there for themselves. My dad, once again, said something to me, years ago, and I didn't understand it then. Now I do. Dad told me, "Jen, you can't find shoes at a hardware store." Finding a soulmate is hard if you don't ask God to show you His choice.

I am not looking in the wrong places anymore; I am trusting God. His will is my will. If I marry, it will be to a

God-fearing Christian man. If God wants me to be single, I will be. After all, I am already His bride. I have found there is a soothing peace when your faith in Jesus becomes stronger than your fear.

*When you change your thoughts,
remember to also change your world.
—Norman Vincent Peale*

Chapter Four

I Have Multiple Sclerosis

Being confident of this, that he who began a good work in you will carry it on to completion until the day of Christ Jesus.
—*Philippians 1:6*

An addict has multiple issues all the time. It is part of the devil's plan to keep them in the clutches of sin and addiction.

I watched Montel Williams on TV. He said he had multiple sclerosis (MS). His symptoms were similar to what I was experiencing. In July 2001 our family was living in Colorado. I went to see my primary physician, who spent two hours with me doing various tests, ruling out this and that. Finally, he looked at me and said, "You already know what I am going to tell you. You more than likely have MS, and an MRI should confirm this." After the MRI, the medical staff confirmed it was MS, my new best friend for the rest of my life, on the 9th of September of the same year.

I was hoping the symptoms would be something else. However, an appointment with an MS specialist confirmed the diagnosis. The doctor treated me like just another common MS patient. Not negative or positive, no genuine support. "Here is a pamphlet, and good luck."

To know about MS, you need to understand the life sentence you are under. Multiple sclerosis is a chronic autoimmune disease that affects the central nervous system. Over time, MS can become a debilitating disease. Many people are constrained by a walker, a wheelchair, or an electric scooter.

Here are some medical facts about MS that will help you understand what I am about to share with you.

MS is more common in women than in men. It's estimated that about 2.3 million people worldwide have MS. And in the United States, women are nearly three times more likely to develop MS than men. Other countries, I imagine, could be different.

MS can occur at any age, but it is most commonly diagnosed between the ages of twenty and fifty. This age range is relevant for women of childbearing age.

The prevalence of MS varies by region in the USA. It's more common in northern states and less common in southern states. This geographical variation is still a subject of research.

MS can cause fatigue, walking problems, numbness, muscle weakness, and coordination difficulties, including forgetfulness. These symptoms can vary in severity and may come and go over your lifetime. Working as a waitress, the coordination and fatigue are a challenge. Then there is forgetfulness. Sometimes you cannot remember how to finish the sentence you just started. Try to remember an order if you have not written it down. Or the customer asks you for something as you are delivering an order. Trust me, this does not work well for you and shows in your tips. I had to stop waitressing. Even being the greeting host became a challenge, as I could not remember which tables I had sat guests at.

MS can progress in different ways, such as relapsing-remitting MS (RRMS), primary progressive MS (PPMS), and secondary progressive MS (SPMS). The course of the disease can vary from person to person. I have RRMS. There are many days I don't know how my body will react. I have woken up not being able to use my legs. Then, in a few hours, I can shuffle and finally walk. Other times I lose focus and cannot clearly see, and that is the reason I didn't drive for many years. If I was scheduled to work, I would try to be there on time and complete my shift. But when you have a hard time walking or seeing, working as wait staff in a restaurant, well, you cannot function. And that doesn't count dropping plates of food or forgetting to place the order for the kitchen to prepare. Hello, unemployment.

Many therapies (and some medications) for MS can slow progression and help manage symptoms. These treatments are often tailored to the individual's specific type of MS and medical history. However, the medications will work for a while, then you will need to switch to another prescription. That will help for a while. You have to keep trying until you find a drug that will work.

The National Multiple Sclerosis Society provides support for MS research. Progress is being made. However, when I see someone who has MS and is using a scooter or wheelchair, I cringe and wonder if or when that will be me. How much time do I have walking on my own?

At this writing, God has blessed me with no further lesions in my brain; for this, I am deeply thankful.

MS affects relationships. My former husband could not understand what was going on with me. He thought it was all in my head, which is accurate, as MS is brain lesions gone wild. But knowing there is not a lot of support from your husband, and sometimes your friends, you just simply take your hits and try to move on, when you can move.

My future could mean using a cane, a walker, or simply not having any coordination of my legs or hands at different times. When I woke up one morning and could not walk, I panicked. I called for help from my former husband, and he said it was because I drank too much the night before. Well, accuracy hits at the heart. But I was afraid I was crippled. I lay there, helpless, with an angry spouse who was correct about my drinking. Alcohol affects my MS, but who cares when you are an addict?

Several hours later, feeling came back to my legs as my hangover headache subsided. Alcohol and MS do not mix, and having my MS dosage discontinued, then changed made for a perfect medical storm. Those stupid decisions of drinking and taking prescription medications—play dumb games, win dumb prizes.

I felt and still feel I am fighting the MS battle almost alone. Some days are better than others. I drop things and forget tasks and requests to do chores or errands. I write lists and then don't remember where I put the lists. All of this makes for an entertaining lifestyle.

I have left my favorite pillow in a hotel room, ear buds on a plane, dinner in the oven, and frozen groceries in a bag on the kitchen counter. Just a lot of continual reminders of forgetfulness from MS.

Then there is the stumbling, falling, missing a step. Going up the steps is not as bad as going down. Tripping can leave a mark for a long time. I have the bruises to prove it. Uneven ground, like grass or dirt, is a dangerous trip factor.

Floors with plush carpet can get me off balance. Solid floors can literally trip me up. An actor from the late 1950s has MS. Many would recognize her from *The Mickey Mouse Club*. The public thought she was drunk. It was her MS. Finally, when her husband revealed her condition, the public and press backed off. When people see me stumble and almost fall, they believe I am drunk. Often I slur my words when these episodes happen. I used this to my advantage when I was drinking. I would blame it on my MS, the medications, or anything else I could use for an excuse.

Once, getting out of the shower, I slipped because I'd forgotten to place the shower mat on the floor. The result was a serious fall and a knee injury that reminds me of that day when the weather makes a change.

Stress can complicate symptoms. When you are in a relationship in which you never know when the next crisis will come up, you cringe at your forgetfulness, your clumsiness. And that really gets to you emotionally as well as physically, as there is little you can do when something happens. Just a simple curb, a small step can tumble your whole day.

However, I have seen people worse off than me. People who cannot walk, have no voice, and depend on a caregiver most if not all of their day. When I encounter an individual who obviously has more challenges than me, I thank my Lord for my condition and say a prayer for the other individual. I know I have mentioned this before, but it is important for me to focus on the positive, not the negative. In the past, being negative was my lifestyle. I was continually the victim.

God's grace and mercy allow me to function. I can drive a car (bike riding is out of the question, as there is that balance issue). I can walk unassisted, without needing a cane, walker, or wheelchair. Stairs are a challenge, but if I move slowly and with caution, I am OK. I have my eyesight, and most of the time I don't drop items. When gravity takes over, it can be entertaining. More fun when you are out in public, however!

Having a support group of family and church family along with my supportive employer allows me to be independent. But there was a time when I played the poor-me card; heck, I used the entire deck!

I was angry at the doctor, mad at the world, and frustrated with my former husband. Most of all, God got the brunt of my over-the-top emotions. Can you tell me why a loving, caring God would do this to *me*? Why would He do anything that involved sorrow and suffering to anyone? Not fair.

I moved away from any form of religion. If I went to church, it was because I was at a recovery center or rehab facility that required attendance. I longed for a relationship with Jesus. I believed in His death and resurrection, and I knew He had saved me, as I had asked Him into my heart early in life. But that didn't mean I had to attend church, study the Bible, or live my life in His will. I would rather be in His face and in His way. The merciful thing is, Jesus continually stayed by my side. Ever patient, ever loving, always there, willing to work with the broken pieces of my life and put me back together.

Of course, I didn't know or realize that in my addictive lifestyle. If you are reading this and it reminds you of a person whom you know is an addict, there is always hope. God never leaves or forsakes us. Sometimes the most powerful action you can take is to pray for that person. Pray with the depth of love Jesus has for you and them. Allow God to work in their lives.

Transformation will not happen overnight, but over time, God willing, you will see results. I know my father, bonus mom, bonus brothers and sister, and so many others continued to pray for me. Simple word, powerful weapon: prayer.

I continued to drink, do drugs, and live a life of a bratty woman who didn't care except where the next cigarette, drink, or fix was coming from. I made sure I was in a crowd that could supply all the above and more.

Let's lock up marriage and throw away the key. I loved my son, but I did him little or no favors while he was growing up. I see that now, and it tears at my heart every day. He has asked me not to contact him, and I get that. Even when I relapsed, I continued to give him hope, only to crush that promise more times than I want to count. I would say it was my MS, but he knew better.

Yet, God, in His grace and mercy, kept me from completely ruining myself. That is why I believe in miracles: because I am His miracle. I am a work in progress, as all of us are. But I am now striving to be in His will, not in His way, as I mentioned before.

Hearing about a life-changing disease can be dealt with in one of two ways. Either you embrace the diagnosis and make the best of the situation, or you get mad, angry, and upset with what you have been told and take your frustration out on people, family, and others around you.

Either way, your life has changed, and your physical and emotional capabilities are now different. So what? You are still you. So which do you choose: be a victim or become a victor? Decide whether to be upset with God or accept your situation and move on, finding the positive in life and embracing what opportunities come your way.

Compared to the apostle Paul's challenges, my multiple sclerosis seems insignificant.

Yet I know I am significant in God's eyes, and that is enough for me.

For the secret of human existence lies not only in living,
but in knowing what to live for.
—Fyodor Dostoevsky

Chapter Five

LIVES LOST

*The Lord is in his holy temple;
the Lord is on his heavenly throne.
He observes everyone on earth;
his eyes examine them.*
—Psalm 11:4

This is my story. Read carefully. I, Jennifer, am not proud of this chapter, but I firmly believe God wants me to tell you this chapter of my life.

There are issues, incidences, and things you don't want your parents to know, ever. We all have secrets we, as children, have kept from our parents. I drank underage. I drove too fast and reckless. Add smoking to the list. There is another deeper, more pressing issue. I stole something I can never return. When you start to steal, you start out with something small and then progress to larger and larger items. I can't recall all the things I pocketed. OK, there are items I did "borrow" when I worked at restaurants. Nothing big, but stealing is stealing. Check the eighth commandment. *You shall not steal.*

The worst, most horrible theft I have repeated twice. I stole two lives, but it was murder as well. I didn't know the depth of sorrowful emotion I would have to deal with now and forever; I am continually paying a lifetime price. Some people have had a greater number of abortions than me, but

I only count my decisions. Regret, yes, sorrow, of course. I cannot change the past. The past has been done; I can only make better decisions in the future. But for those who are totally defenseless, they have no choice in a fatal decision. Such was the case with my choice to end two lives before they had a chance at life outside the womb.

Every day, when I see a mother with a newborn, a precious life, I wonder about the lives I agreed to cancel before they (he and/or she, I don't know) had a chance of taking even one breath. Does that make me a killer? Yes. Do I feel the depth of sorrow about my decision? Definitely. Would I change my life path back then? Of course. What I did was morally wrong. Consenting to sex (and that was all it was) before marriage was totally not a decision I would make now.

Despite my discomfort and lack of pride in this chapter of my life, it is necessary to recount what happened. This will not be gentle; I will be honest, honest to a fault, because if you are considering abortion, you need to reconsider. There are many other options. However, let me be clear. If you don't play around or put yourself in a position to be pregnant, then a choice like I made will not be part of your life.

I had my first sexual encounter at fifteen with Frank on prom night, but he wasn't even my date for the night! Funny, I thought he liked me, and I proved my affection for him in one way, the wrong way. I know now you don't have to prove anything to anyone. They should know from your actions and commitment. Committing to sex is not proof, and that is abundantly clear in the Bible. Read the seventh commandment. *You shall not commit adultery.*

Believe me when I say having premarital sex is not the thrill that you think it is. The media's deception on this issue is unfair to impressionable minds. The unsuspecting individual really believes in embracing this thought pattern, especially when an unborn life is conceived. And there is the sixth commandment. *You shall not commit murder.*

I first got pregnant when I was nineteen. (I thought I was probably pregnant.) Well, there is not a *probably* in pregnancy, whether you are or are not. I was, and I needed to figure out what to do. But who do you talk to when your stepdad is an abuser and your mother is difficult to communicate with? That left my dad, and I would not tell him. I knew what his answer would be. And that would be to bring the baby to full term. I believe he and his wife would have raised the child as their own. However, I didn't see that as an option. This was my issue, my problem, and I would figure out a solution that I already knew would not be physically or emotionally comfortable for me. It took a while to come to this decision, and then there was money; it is always about dollars. John and I had to pay for the procedure.

Trying to talk to the guy who got me in this situation was a travesty. He said he would marry me and we would raise the child. I didn't want to spend the rest of my life with him. That brings up the question, why this evening tryst? Can you tell me why I even spent an evening with him? I was out of control; I knew that, but an addict doesn't have a lot of control over wants, fixes, situations, or solutions.

John did not agree with my decision for marriage or an abortion. He called me a "baby killer," and he was right. I wish I could tell you why he took me to the center. I don't know.

Finally, we came to an agreement that I would abort the child and he would take me to the clinic. We would both contribute to the expense. It seemed so easy. Go, have the procedure, then go home as if nothing happened. I had little or no feelings for this life growing and living in me, so I thought this would be just another notch to add to my addiction life story.

This became more than just a notch. When you have an abortion, you are killing a life. However, you are also taking part of your life and throwing it away. Nothing can be reversed. A procedure is more than that.

Walking into an abortion clinic seems like a simple step; however, each step becomes harder. My feet felt as heavy as lead, and every step became heavier and heavier.

The receptionist was all smiles, welcoming me to the most crucial and desecrating decision I have made and will ever make. I was there with other women, or maybe couples. "The nurse will be with you in a few minutes," I heard the smiley receptionist say. I looked around, but my life was a blur, visual and secret tears tore at my soul. Holding John's hand was like holding smoke. Emotion was void. This place was the personification of evil. I could feel the evil throughout my body, seeping into my bones.

Unlike most other waiting rooms, the noncommittal ambiance of the waiting room was clear. The atmosphere was not one of healing, like a doctor's office or counseling center can be. The program claimed to offer counseling, but in reality, their support was solely focused on one objective: abortion. Abortion, then move on.

I felt cold, uncaring, nervous, ashamed, complacent, wrong. If my heavy feet would have carried me, I would have run out of the killing waiting room. But I believed I was stuck. I had made a fatal decision to end a life that had not begun. I wanted to cry, scream, yell, "This procedure is incorrect on all levels." But I sat there, mute, hands folded, like an animal being led to slaughter. And that was exactly what I was doing.

Frozen shards of ice ran through my veins. *What choice do I have?* I thought. My mom supported me and had offered to take me to the clinic to support my fatal decision. I knew Dad and my bonus mom would have taken the newborn (soon to be unborn) baby and raised it for and with me. The thought of saving and giving a life spun in my brain. But John would be involved, or so I thought. In retrospect, I believe John would have bolted at the first request to change a dirty, stinky diaper or clean up after the baby.

But I didn't think any of those thoughts were a solution. My thoughts came to a screeching halt as the nurse called my name. "Jennifer, we are ready for you." She was ready. I was not. As I looked around, I now realized I had been sitting with other women who were there for the same reason. The room finally came into focus. It was like any other reception room. Magazines that were not being read, girls there with their boyfriends or a family relative. We were all alone, sitting and looking down, not knowing what was coming next. I wondered what they were thinking. There was no one with a smile, just a defeated look of sorrow and sadness. I believe God works full-time in this room. His sorrow at the decision I made, along with all the others, pains Him deeply. Perhaps as deep as when He turned His face away from His Son as Jesus died on the cross. As I shuffled out of the reception area, I noticed some men were sitting there alone. Some showed emotion, others, nothing.

Recent studies show that individuals between the ages of nineteen and thirty undergo abortions. Guess I fit that profile. Here are the facts on abortion from Pew Research Center:

> "In the District of Columbia and the 46 states that reported age data to the CDC in 2021, the majority of women who had abortions (57%) were in their 20s, while 31% were in their 30s. Teens ages 13 to 19 accounted for 8% of those who had abortions, while women ages 40 to 44 accounted for about 4%.

> "The vast majority of women who had abortions in 2021 were unmarried (87%), while married women accounted for 13%, according to the CDC, which had data on this from 37 states."[3]

They escorted me into a room and instructed me to lie on a cold, unforgiving table. I was told to take my clothes off and don a hospital robe. My mind raced back to the time of conception. I had willingly disrobed, and look what happened. Now I was doing it again, this time in front of medical strangers who didn't care. Well, maybe John didn't care either; it was just a score for him. I know now it was a fatal mistake for me and my unborn baby, yet there I was. Naked physically, emotionally numb, and nude with my thoughts and "our" decision.

I looked over at the wall, looked at the ceiling, my eyes blurred with untold tears of the coming regret and sorrow I knew I would soon feel even more. This emotion, I believe, was the Holy Spirit crying out to God, who was also weeping about what was about to happen. What was supposed to be a temporary pleasure was now turning into a forever sorrow. A tear slid down my face. The nurse and the doctor said nothing. I knew they had both seen my tears, my saddened look. This was just another killing, one more of many for that day.

There was a nurse and an abortion doctor for each procedure. "This won't take long," said the doctor, and the sound of the suction machine started up. "Take a deep breath and try to distract yourself." The machine spun rapidly, amplifying the noise of material being torn away from my body. And I lay there feeling the numbing killing of a life I will not know until heaven. "Lord, forgive me," I prayed, knowing I could not possibly forgive myself. Silent internal tears cascaded down, burning into my soul, and then the pain became more than emotional; it became physical.

My soul numbed at the sounds in the room. "Almost finished," I heard someone say. *No,* I thought, *not finished. This is forever.* A life lost and a life forever changed, and no one tells you about the emotional and physical pain.

"All done. You can get dressed now," the doctor said as he snapped off the surgical gloves he had been wearing. *No, nothing is all done.* I knew in my heart I would never be the same. My decision had taken a life, a life that was defenseless, a beating heart ripped apart, the body shredded, limb by limb. Now a living human body, gone, yet a soul in heaven.

The doctor stood up and left the room, acting as if nothing had happened. Just another paycheck for him. The nurse was cleaning up the suction machine (mushed body parts within). She shielded it from me, but I knew what was in there. She said nothing. I was sore, numb. Then she left the room. I was alone, then the power went out. Welcome to darkness in more than one way. There was no follow-up about the physical pain I sensed I would feel soon enough. No support, just put your clothes back on, walk out of the room, go down the hallway. I passed the receptionist. I looked at her, daring her to tell me to have a nice rest of my day.

John said nothing, didn't hold me or my hand. I walked, well, shuffled to the car. On the drive home, John's car broke down. He could push the vehicle. I had just had a life sucked out of me, and my life sucked. I broke down, but I wouldn't let John see my tears. He had seen enough already.

What would this child have been if I hadn't made that killing decision? Whom did I destroy by making that fatal choice? I pray for the baby's forgiveness. I know God has forgiven me, but can I forgive myself?

The emotional impact of taking a life leaves a void in your soul that never disappears. My decision is a life sentence for me, for a life that never formed a sentence.

I recall walking out of that abortion clinic feeling not relieved, not happy, only feeling numb to the world. Numb emotionally, physically. I was in pain, lots of mental and physical pain. They don't tell you that before the procedure. You find out about that on your own. Welcome to reality. Welcome to the knowledge of a life lost that, at the most, only six people would know about. Receptionist, nurse, doctor, mother, "boyfriend," and yourself. This is a secret you will carry with you forever.

Yet now, as I reflect on the two abortions I have had, I find the mercy and grace of God. The first time didn't teach me; I learned I could be weak and go with decisions that were not right but were morally wrong. I learned that instant pleasure can and will bring sustaining bondage. Bondage in your emotions and reactions.

What was it like the first time I saw a newborn after my never-born decision? I cannot tell you; I feel I avoided looking at babies. I know I would not hold a baby until I had my one and only child. But I don't hold him now or talk to him today. (That is another story for another time.)

Healing from an abortion is never complete. You always wonder what could have been, what was and is not now. I am grateful that someone adopted my dad. She chose a different path than me, but I was able to meet my bio-grandmother, a reunion of acceptance and love. Two souls will not know any earthly family, but I firmly believe they have an eternal family and someday I will meet them. There will be no words that I can offer. I can only ask for their forgiveness, which I believe they have already given me.

I must work, every day, on my personal forgiveness. And that forgiveness process takes a small baby step every day. My soul will heal, sometime, but if there is a reason for this chapter, it is this: writing about what happened was a cathartic procedure. A secret kept way too long, now revealed, now known. This part of my life has been difficult to write, but the story is out now, and I pray it will help others. That is all I expect.

God has fearfully and wonderfully created you. He has a purpose for your life. Perhaps you know what that purpose in His will is. Maybe you do not. Yet you are reading this chapter. There is a reason for you seeing these words. I encourage you to seek His will and to listen to His Holy Spirit's voice. If you feel something is incorrect, it is. Run, run as if another life depends on it, because it does.

May I offer this prayer for you?

Precious Heavenly Father, You have given us life, precious life. Help those who are contemplating taking a silent life. Alleviate their worries, provide solace in their grief, and empower them to embrace the precious gift of bringing a new life into the world. Surround them with love and support to lighten their heavy burden. Dear Lord, please shine Your merciful light on them so that they may see Your love. Bring them happiness in their child, and give them the wisdom and insight to lead their future family. Allow this future mother to know that the love You have for her extends to her child. And if she gives this precious life up for adoption, be with the new family and bless them beyond measure.

Help heal the mother's wounded heart. Intercede on behalf of each of them. May this parent receive the ability to raise this child with self-sacrificing love, mirroring Your example. We ask this through Christ our Lord. Amen.

*To forgive is the highest, most beautiful form of love.
In return, you will receive untold peace and happiness.*
—Robert Muller

Chapter Six

ANOTHER CRISIS AND CONFLICT

*Trust in the Lord with all your heart
and lean not on your own understanding;
in all your ways submit to him,
and he will make your paths straight.
—Proverbs 3:5–6*

Dad's Story - October 2009

My wife, Barb, and I were traveling back to Colorado when I received a distressing phone call from Jennifer. "Come and get me. I am in danger, and I don't think I am safe here." She was calling from the Fort Lauderdale area, where I expected she was doing OK, not the best, just OK. At first, I thought, *Trauma drama.* But after consulting with and listening to other family members, they recommended I go to her immediately. I left the next day to see what was going on and why all the drama.

My flight arrived after dark in Fort Lauderdale, and I found my way to her place. It was a mess, full of cockroaches and trash, with personal items all over the bungalow, which could have been a cute place to live, but not now. She feared for her safety, continually looking out the window, even though she could see nothing because of the lack of streetlights.

"He won't come back as long as you are here," Jennifer stated about her drug dealer, who I had found out had threatened her life. Protecting my daughter was foremost on my mind. I found a PVC pipe that would work as a bat if he returned. Sweeping his kneecaps would incapacitate him, and then the police would be involved. I didn't care. I could clearly see that Jennifer was not safe in Florida. She needed to leave. She needed help to do that.

Calling her mother, who lived in the Florida Keys, was the next step. I asked her to come and help clean out the bungalow and see her daughter. Although they didn't have the best of relationships, I hoped having the two of them together would help them reconcile, at least a little.

Her mom did show up to help. I believe it was difficult for her mom to see the living tragedy that Jennifer had become. Many trips were made to the local secondhand store. Memories were given away, lost, or left in the bungalow.

I had rented the largest car I could find, and we loaded up as many of Jennifer's belongings as we could. We gave away so many family things, but it was important to leave as quickly as possible. There was no telling when this drug dealer would return and what the result would be.

Our drive back to Colorado took several days, and Jennifer slept the whole way. I thought we could talk and maybe listen to some Christian instructional lessons on turning your life around, but that didn't happen. Jennifer slept all day and then all night. Trauma and addiction do that to a person. However, as we traveled mile upon mile away from her danger, I believed she was safer.

Our plan was to support Jennifer, to bring her back into a loving family. Perhaps this would be a chance to start anew and leave the past behind. However, with a drug addict who is looking for their next fix, their next high or low, the plans you have, the hopes that you have for a better drug-free life for them, are plans that rarely come to fruition.

For a while, things seemed to be on the upswing, but within several weeks, Jennifer had found a drug source, a doctor who prescribed downers for her. She was smoking cigarettes or weed again and would volunteer to check the mailbox a few hundred yards from our house. You can figure out why she did that.

Her demeanor changed gradually each day. She made less contact, slept more, had no interaction with anyone: clear behaviors of an addict, which started controlling our lives. One day, Barb discovered Jennifer's drug use and gave me an ultimatum. Barb said, "Jennifer needs more than we or this community can give her. AA isn't working. Church has little or no effect on her. Either she goes or I go."

I was gut punched, run over by a wave of grief. Dads sometime don't see the entire picture, and I was definitely not seeing the deplorable condition Jennifer was in. Reality checks hit hard, and tough love from spouse to spouse can be an emotional bullet between the eyes when you are at the corner of love and denial.

Jen needed more help than we could provide. While we could provide emotional and financial support, we weren't equipped to guide her through her addiction recovery.

Barb and I looked for a place that was equipped with the Christian spiritual and healing tools we felt she needed. After many hours searching the Internet, we were led to Teen Challenge in Texas, further away than I wanted. Trusting our Lord is sometimes very difficult, as you cannot see over the horizon, yet God sees and knows the loving answer. We also confronted the doctor, who said she didn't realize Jennifer was an addict. (That is just how well an addict can conceal their addiction.)

We told Jennifer she needed more help than we could give, and that we knew about her getting the prescription drugs from the doctor.

We said we had a place for her to go and that we would leave the next day. The storm started when she said she would not go but would find another place to live if we didn't love her enough to let her stay with us. We responded that she was going to be placed into a facility that could help her.

Jennifer called every person she could think of, asking if she could stay with them. The answer was always "no." That tactic didn't work. Her friends were aware of her addiction, or they didn't have a place. I believe all the calls were negative because God knew the help she required and where she needed to be treated.

Then an ultimatum came from Jennifer. She agreed to be admitted to Teen Challenge if she could see her son in Florida. (We had all talked to the intake counselor, and they promised there would be a bed for her.) It would take us over a week to arrive in Florida. Jennifer didn't think we would agree to the extended trip, but we departed the next day as planned.

Our commitment was to get help for our addicted youngest daughter, and if it took her seeing her son, Kaleb, that would be part of the agreement.

We were off on a learning "adventure." And learn we did. It is amazing the mind of an addict and the ways and means they can come up with to fuel their habit. The first night we stopped close to a national discount store, and Jennifer said she needed a few things. An hour later, she was back. We never saw what the few things were. We realized we could not trust her out of our sight anymore. From then on, we drove from early morning into the night and stayed in rural, out-of-the-way rest stops. We camped in unsafe areas to keep Jennifer safe and away from any opportunity to purchase drugs.

Traveling to Florida took five days. We only had one day to see Kaleb. We were in an RV park where Jennifer and her eight-year-old son could swim and simply hang out. Although the reunion was bittersweet, I believe it was necessary, not only for Jennifer but for Kaleb as well, to see there was hope in the future for his mom. However, the conversation between Jennifer and Kaleb's dad was one of the usual with fiery words, accusations, and mistrust.

Arriving at Teen Challenge (TC) was the end of one journey and the start of another for all of us. The facility for TC women was a house in a typical downtown Texas oil town. Built in the late 1940s, it was an average size house, with a welcoming atmosphere. We rang the doorbell, and another rehabilitation process began as Jennifer crossed the threshold.

After Jennifer was admitted, the staff asked us to stay for lunch. Once she was in the program, we could not have any contact with Jennifer for a month. When it was time to leave, we said a prayer of thanksgiving, hugged, and teared up, and I held her hand as long as I could. The staff gently opened the main door, signaling it was time for us to depart and for Jennifer's journey to begin. Barb and I walked over the threshold, hearing the door creak as the door shut. My last image of Jennifer was of her just inside the door, tears in her eyes, beginning her journey. She was in the hands of God, who would protect Teen Challenge, their counselors, clients, and support staff. We had delivered her, hopefully, to a new beginning, again, for the first time . . . again.

Jennifer's Story

I can and will get myself in a mess; as a matter of fact, in some ways I have developed it into an art form. I have been told that I come close to the finish line of anything I do and then don't cross it. I am not a finisher. Such is the life of an addict.

I wasn't exaggerating when I called my daddy and said, "Come and pick me up. I'm in danger and I feel unsafe." The guy I was hanging out with was dangerous. The Delray police knew him as a drug dealer, and I was hosting him at my place. He was violent, and yet I continued the relationship. That is me, settling for less in relationships and trying to make more out of the relationship than can ever be. In thinking about the relationship, there really wasn't one. I was being used.

Hearing that Daddy was coming to rescue me (again) gave me hope and maybe a restart for a better life. A life without drugs and dangerous friends. A life focused on Jesus. That was what I wanted, but that was not what happened.

I remember a little about traveling to my daddy's home. I slept. He drove. We would have a meal together and then I would sleep. Addicts do a lot of sleeping. I felt bad (not that bad) about not being awake during our trip to Colorado. We lost a great deal of personal sharing time, as I was still under the influence of drugs, which I had taken before we started traveling.

After a few weeks of being safe in my daddy and bonus mom's home, I was looking for whatever I could swallow. The withdraws were demons demanding attention in my soul. They were pounding to get released with the floating feeling of not feeling anything. I knew I could get something, anything, if I could see a medical professional. I told my dad I was not feeling well and needed to see a doctor. He scheduled an appointment for me the same day, and I got some downers. I could sleep all day and be restless in the dark hours because my dark hours were all hours of the day. Success, or so I thought.

Barbie (my nickname for my daddy's wife) is no Sherlock Holmes, but darn close. She saw the downward progression in my personality and my interaction with family. Then she saw what I was taking. You can get information on the Internet, and Barbie's research revealed that I was on things I didn't need. Busted, discovered, held accountable.

Then the family crap hit the fan. Dad and Barbie sat me down and said I could not stay here at this safe place, doing what I was doing. I denied I was hooked, saying that I just needed my meds to make it through the day. (I am such a liar.) The more I protested, the stronger their resolve became. I had no choice but to go to Teen Challenge. Not happening, not going. I called anyone and everyone I knew, and not one person would take me in. (Thank you, God, for that direction and protection in my life.)

I was angry at my dad for his unified front with Barbie. I was mad at Barbie because she was the one who busted me and placed me in this rehab ultimatum. They caught me and found me guilty. Actions have consequences, but I still believed I was above all consequences and that I could talk my way out of this conflict and stay in the home I had never known. That didn't happen.

I stormed around the house as they prepared to take me to a place I didn't know. A place I didn't want to go to because I didn't need what Teen Challenge offered. What was Teen Challenge anyway? I was way, way past being a teenager.

The intake counselor informed me that there was a space available but that they could fill it in a week. My plan was, I would go, but I wanted to see my son, Kaleb, in Florida first. I thought they would say no and I would not have to go to Teen Challenge, or we would get there, and the space would not be available. Well, that didn't work. TC agreed to hold the space for me, and we would go back to Fort Lauderdale to see Kaleb for a day. That tactic was unsuccessful, and we were off in the RV. The first night, I manipulated my way into a store; they caught on to my routine, and from then on, we never stayed where I could score, so I slept the entire trip. (I thought that would show them.)

Seeing my son, whom I really had not raised but for just a brief time, was a blessing. Leaving him, knowing I would not see him for over a year, was a tear in my heart, but that was another consequence of my addiction.

If I was not sleeping, I was reading and thinking of ways to get something, even cigarettes. Those I had, but a limited amount. There was no smoking at TC; I was going to prison as far as I was concerned. I imagined a lot of negative things. Would I be in a uniform with "TC" emblazoned on the back? Would it be the jailhouse orange you always hear about? How much privacy would there be? Would I be able to escape? All I wanted was a way to get out and score something.

My last night before entering TC, we stayed in an RV campground and went out to dinner (last supper for me, as far as I was concerned). I didn't sleep well. Could I just sneak out and disappear? There was a plan. I was too afraid, and I didn't know where we were, just in the great state of Texas. I had not paid attention to our location. There was nowhere to go except Teen Challenge.

Arriving at the facility was interesting. It was a house! Not some square institutional building. I thought, *Well, this differs from other places I have been. This doesn't look like the usual type of intervention rehab center.*

I could tell Dad was in a somber mood. Barbie was too, and yet she had everything organized for me. She had taken the time to supply me with vitamin supplements to help me. I never said "thank you" for her caring and direction. So, thank you now, Barbie. I realize you always wanted to help me, and part of that help was getting me the support I didn't think I needed. When I reflect, I wonder about all the prayers you said on my behalf. Again, thank you.

We knocked on the door and waited. I hoped no one was there. The door swung open with a creaking sound, and I thought, *Well, there goes that chance for a quiet escape*, and my life started in another direction. Entering the house, I could see I was not the only person who was not in their teen years. Surprise, surprise.

Filling out the intake forms was a chore but a necessary part of the process. I could not believe the drug form where it asked to check the "have you ever used or taken" this and that substance. There were thirty-five drugs listed. I checked twenty-seven of them! Maybe I needed help, but I still didn't think so. Denial, a crutch for an addict, and I had more than one pair of crutches.

After I filled all the forms out, they asked all of us to stay for lunch. I was not hungry, and then the dad of all dads said yes, we would like to stay. I was thankful for the extra time. What I observed was the way the other clients engaged my dad in conversations about the Bible, Jesus, Jesus's life, and the impact He had on the world. Maybe this Jesus thing, whom I had asked into my heart, was not just for Sundays anymore. Not that I went to church—I didn't—but I recognized there was something very special about Jesus. Yet the devil kept at me to not allow His saving grace.

After lunch was finished, it was time for Dad and Barbie to leave. Stalling was not doing any good. We said our goodbyes several times. I knew I could not talk to family or anyone for a month. We walked to the door, and I stood there as the door creaked closed. Dad and Barbie were on the other side, gone. The door shut and my time with Teen Challenge started. This was Monday, a "quiet out" day. We could only talk when we dined. I desperately wanted to talk to the other clients, but that would not happen until the next day. I was alone with sixteen other women in a silent world. Assigned to a bed, a desk. They gave me my belongings after they searched through them (there went my last cigarettes and lighter). I was alone with my thoughts. This journey had started for the first time or sixth time. I could not remember. At least the bed was comfortable.

Be sure you put your feet in the right place, then stand firm.
—Abraham Lincoln

Chapter Seven

TEEN CHALLENGE

I will never leave you nor forsake you.
—Joshua 1:5

Dad's Story

To understand Teen Challenge, it is important to know its beginning and history.

Reverend David Wilkerson started this Christian organization in 1958. He left his safe country church, where he was pastor, to go to Hell's Kitchen in New York City to minister to gang members. When he had read an article in *Life* magazine about a murder by teenage gangs, David Wilkerson heard God speak: "Go to New York City and help those boys." They were on trial for murder. Since the challenging, humble beginnings of Teen Challenge, the organization has grown to over 200 locations in the United States and 1,000 internationally.

Teen Challenge has the philosophy of exchanging weapons for Bibles. TC's focus is to bring people to Christ. Not an easy job, but one that Wilkerson embraced because of God's direction, and so a ministry was born.

Wilkerson released his book *The Cross and the Switchblade* in February 1963, and people have bought over 50 million copies. Millions of people have read the book and seen the movie, and the movie has been translated into over thirty languages since its opening in 1972. Founder David Wilkerson was promoted to heaven on April 27th, 2011, in a tragic head-on collision.

From early on, TC has commissioned studies to find out the recovery rate of their graduates. Consistently, these studies have shown a success rate between 67 and 84 percent, thus making the TC programs and curriculum one of the most successful to release teens and adults from addiction.

However, some resist the gift that TC offers and leave the program or re-offend with their habit. Jennifer was one of those who got snagged in the net of further addiction. Yet, as you continue to read, you will see that TC roots run deep in people and the teaching continues in individuals who have been in the program. There is a verse in Proverbs that states, "Start children off on the way they should go, and even when they are old they will not turn from it" (Proverbs 22:6). Jennifer was raised in a "Christian lite" family. Going to TC helped reinforce her Christian upbringing and beliefs. But addiction is a jealous companion and will continue to hold on to a person by any means possible. So the story continues.

Jennifer's Story

A comfortable bed, yes, but I was not allowed to be on the bed during the day. I was required to be in meetings, studying, doing something. Wonderful. Just what the doctor didn't order. I thought I would be the oldest person in this program. I thought Teen Challenge would be a bunch of immature teenagers experimenting with life for the first time. How wrong I was. The women in the program ranged in age from teenagers to women in their fifties. Addiction doesn't respect age. That alone was a revelation to me. I realized if I didn't get clean, the addictions I had would be a lifetime sentence. (In retrospect, that was still going to be the case. More on that later.)

They inspected, washed, and gave back almost all of the personal items I had brought into the house, the exceptions being some lighters and other contraband I thought I could sneak in. Along with my clothes and personal items being checked, so it was with me too. Can you say "strip search?" Now, that is completely humiliating. I thought, *I will never get to a point where I will have to go through that again.* Just goes to show, you can't predict the future.

The home we were in was ancient, built in the 1940s, but nice. TC staff was caring and considerate, unless you didn't follow the rules. Staff would dole out consequences if you did not adhere to the rules. They held you accountable for all your actions, something new for me. I could always get by with less, but that was not the case here.

Our daily schedule was something of a boring but necessary routine. We would be awakened in the morning and were required to make our bed before breakfast. The morning meal was wonderful. I had never had breakfasts like this unless I went out. Having a drug or alcohol hangover doesn't make you want to go for breakfast. The smell of bacon grease, fried eggs, and pancake syrup are odors not welcome when you are nursing a throbbing headache and have an upset, churning, gurgling stomach.

Many of the residents called Teen Challenge "Bible Boot Camp," and that was accurate. We were required to read and study the Bible. Then there was the cleaning of churches. That is how TC receives support money. Cleaning God's house angered me. Actually, everything angered me. No drugs meant I could not smoke cigarettes or anything else. Booze was not allowed. Oh, joy. We would study, clean, read, talk, sleep, and start over. Every Sunday was church. It seemed like every day was church, and I was not pleased with my new lifestyle.

However, I was here, and God was working overtime on my life, although I didn't know it. I found comfort in the camaraderie of the residents and the staff and felt the unconditional love and support from TC staff and the women I met at church. All of this was new to me. Addiction isolates you, keeps you in the clutches of the evil one. Here, at TC, there was a comfort I had not known since living with my dad.

The main campus is called The Farm. It is on a plot of land that was donated for redirecting lost lives. To state you are out in the country is accurate. Surrounding the farm are country houses, oil wells, and some businesses. Town is north of the farm and seven miles away. Some clients "rabbit" and walk off, thinking life will be better for them without direction. Many of these rabbits are never heard from again.

After a few months, we were moved to a new facility on The Farm. A new women's shelter had been built. Each room had its own shower! There was a larger dining room, a wonderful living room, and laundry. Luxury! I thought, *If this is God working, well, that is something.* I was being softened to His presence and His will. Once a week, we had evening chapel where the men and the women would gather. Women on one side, men on the other. A special speaker would give a sermon, and there would be singing and prayer but no interaction with the guys, except for sideways glances casually taken.

My dad came to visit me at TC. Barbie (bonus mom) was there to support me, support that was hard for me to accept. One time, she made the evening meal for all the girls: my favorite, enchiladas. I loved her (at a distance) for that meal. I could not believe with all the hurt and sorrow I had put her and my dad through that Barbie would spend the time, the effort, to do this for me. Perhaps I was learning something. Learning about unconditional love, learning about how Jesus would treat me, a sinner.

I was asked if I could drive the TC van and take the cleaning team to the churches we were tasked with cleaning. That was a new thing for me: trust with a vehicle of value. I received my Texas driver's license and was officially a TC driver. As I continued in the eight-to-twelve month program that lasted fifteen months for me, I was given more responsibilities and freedom. The freedom part got me into trouble.

But before that, my mom came to visit me for a week and brought my son. He was ten and full of adventure. What a joy it was to see how much he had grown and matured. Hearing him call me Mama was a delight. We had a wonderful week of card playing, laughing, and family time. The week went way too fast, but the memories were there.

On The Farm was a house that was used for transitioning. From the women's facility, I moved up to the transition house. This was graduation for me. One more step, and I would be on my own, independent of TC and out in the world. I had my own room at last! I had a job in town; independence was within my reach.

Dad and Barbie came down and helped me make my room mine, all mine. What a wonderful feeling to have personal space. A place for just me. I was feeling prideful, and that is not the best feeling. Thankful, yes; pride, that is dangerous.

They say pride goes before the fall. Accurate. I started looking for a guy, and I found several who, again, took advantage of me, my income, my body, and my mind. Hello and welcome back, drugs, which got me kicked out of TC and all the support I still needed. Once again, the evil one reinforced my feeling that I had failed again. I was welcomed back to the opening of the emotional miry pit, and I slid back down into darkness.

Leaving Teen Challenge was, to me, another failure in a lifetime of regret and continued negative circumstances. I had failed at marriage, raising my son, and many jobs. (I could almost predict when I was going to be fired.) Everything I did fouled up every relationship I had with men. Even cooking was a failure. If I could have, I would have even burned water. That was my life. Yet God, in His grace and mercy, continued to shelter me. He continued to love me, even though that was something I didn't do for myself.

I applied and was accepted for subsidized housing. I would have a one-bedroom apartment, and rent would be based on my income, which was not much. Again, I would have my own special place. Many of the ladies at a church I used to attend became "Team Jennifer." They found furniture, dishes, and other items for my place. I had "agreed" not to use any illegal drugs, as that was reason to be evicted. Like that was going to not happen. Drugs were my meal of choice.

Dad and Barbie came to visit me one Thanksgiving. We had a wonderful holiday meal. Barbie fixed all the food for this family day. We even went to church that following Sunday. We were family. And bonus, they brought me a TV, and I had a DVD player. My brother-in-law had given me a computer. I had a job with benefits and steady hours. Life was good, but, remember, I have a bad picker with boy "friends." And I never picked carefully. Each choice turned out to be worse than the previous one. I was on a roll. Satan was, again, in charge, and the prison pit was being made ready for me.

I was a doormat, and the drug community knew it. Because I stole from my job, I was fired; gone was my promising future in corporate America. I took one job after another, being let go of each one. Drugs became, once again, my source of numbing the hurt. And friendships from church fell off because I didn't want "Team Jennifer" to see what I was becoming, well, had become. Each day was a hunt for a fix of some kind.

Then a "girlfriend" (drug supplier would be accurate) said she needed a place to stay for "just a few days." That was against the lease agreement I had signed, but I didn't care. Rules were to be bent and broken. I believed there would be no consequences. Wrong. The few days turned into over a week.

You know how you get those Holy Spirit feelings? I felt something was not right. One day, she kept hanging around, and I needed to get to work. She was supposed to leave before I went to my job. Finally, I left and told her to leave the apartment key I had given her on the table. She kept saying her ride would show up. Well, the ride showed up as a truck with several people with sticky, stealing hands. I came home for lunch, wanting to be sure she was gone and my key was there. She was gone, along with my TV, computer, cosmetics, sheets, and many other things. Welcome to the world of drug friends. At least the key was there, but did they make a copy? Would they be back for more things, or for me? My world was shattered again.

Things are stuff, and stuff can be replaced. Personal invasion and stealing cuts to the mire of your soul. I felt more unclean than I ever had. The feelings of being invaded, in danger, and violated overflowed my emotions, like white water over a dam. I needed some kind of fix, something strong. There is an answer that can kill you, and I wanted to be dead. Life was not going my way, but I was not going Jesus's way, so go figure. Actions have consequences, and my decisions to be a nice doormat and to listen to a sad sob story resulted in me trusting the wrong people.

I called my dad. He listened with a sympathetic voice, but I could tell he could see this was just another part of my life ending in a more than negative way. Sitting in my invaded apartment, looking around, and seeing the loss drove me closer and closer to just calling it quits. But God held my heart and extended His hand to hold my trembling hand. I saw this incident as another failure. Another nail in my coffin of low self-esteem. This was a big nail, maybe the last nail needed.

I should have never done the things that caused Teen Challenge to ask me to leave. I needed the loving support of the staff at TC, but that was now not an option. That chapter of my life, for now, was closed. Little did I know I would be back at the TC farm in a few years!

The lesson I learned from my possessions being taken was not learned well, because it happened again, but not like this time. I gave trust away freely, hoping for acceptance and friendship. I know better now. Trust is something people have to earn from you.

In the next chapter, I relate how I made a life-changing decision that impacted my life for two years. This is something you never want to be a part of.

Pride is the sin most likely to keep you
from crying out to your Savior.
—*John Boyer*

Chapter Eight

GOING TO PRISON

*So do not fear, for I am with you;
do not be dismayed, for I am your God.
I will strengthen you and help you;
I will uphold you with my righteous right hand.
—Isaiah 41:10*

Jennifer's Story - November 2013

I know I should not have agreed to get in the car. We were to go from Midland, Texas, to Artesia, New Mexico. Traveling with the two girls to purchase drugs they would sell was simply stupid. I had just finished a call from my dad, said goodnight, and told him I was going to go to bed too. We talked just about every night. I did not know I would have only one phone call the next morning to say they had arrested me on drug charges.

We drove into the night. Night is the best time: there is less law enforcement out, or so you would think. The gals let me off at a fast-food place that was open all night because I told them I didn't want to be a part of the transaction. They went and did their illegal transaction. The entire trip, I had an uneasy feeling about going. Can you tell me why I went? I still cannot answer, except that a guy friend had promised to come over and hadn't. I felt rejected. After all, a promise is a promise. Agreeing to go was a stupid mistake. That decision became a Rubicon turning point in my life, one that I would like to rewind in the VCR version of my life—erase and forget.

During the drive to score drugs, there was that nagging feeling of warning that the evening would not turn out well for any of us. As we traveled the miles, my concern and fear that something terrible was going to happen grew deeper and deeper. I know now this was the Holy Spirit telling me, but I didn't listen to that thundering velvet voice. Going with these two dealers was a mistake. I wasn't a dealer—a consumer, yes, a dealer, no—so what the heck was I doing tagging along? They say hindsight is crystal clear, and that is accurate. Thinking back, I should have told the girls I was going to stay at the fast-food place and then figured a way to get back to my apartment. I didn't, and we were on our way back to Texas.

Driving back into Midland was a relief. We were home. We had gotten by with an illegal transaction. I was going home to sleep, or so I thought. Then the night lit up with flashing lights, sirens, and a command to pull over. I was in denial, just a taillight out, that is what I thought. Not so, not even close. It was the Midland police who had been sitting on the side of the road, observing and watching. They said we didn't use our turn signal.

The Midland police knew the two girls I was with. They knew of me, and it surprised the police when they saw me with the two girls. Because they knew the reputation of the girls, the Midland drug force was called. That resulted in us sitting on the curb, handcuffed, red and blue lights flashing from the police cars—and I had thought we were home free. I was uncuffed, and I thought, *I am done here!* That was not in their plan.

Going to Prison

When the police re-cuffed me—and it was a shock—I knew then I was going to jail. I planted my feet in fear, unbelief, and defiance. Two of the officers picked me up by my arms and moved me into the police cruiser. I could not quit sobbing. Even though I had lived with police officers (stepdad and mother), handcuffing was something that had not happened in our house; this was not a laughing matter. This emotionally devastated me. Never in my life had I thought this would happen to me. I was above all of this, and rules didn't apply to my life, just to others. Being handcuffed, arrested, driven to booking, and then placed in a cell was a 100 percent reality check for me. I knew I would not get out of this situation lightly.

They placed us in the Midland jail for the evening. The cell was cold and stark, with no feeling of welcome. I could hear the metal clanging of doors being locked and unlocked all night. Sleep was not an option.

The next day, the US Marshal's office came and took me to the county lockup. For the second time, I heard the cold, unfriendly metallic slamming of jail doors being shut on me. I could not stop crying. I was emotionally devastated, which resulted in me slashing my wrists. The guards had given us a disposable razor along with other hygiene items (why a razor?). That stunt got me placed in a solitary cell with no mattress on the stainless steel bed, but there was a shelf on the wall. I was alone, scared. I continued to bawl my eyes out. Honestly, I didn't think anyone could have that many tears. Because I was now on suicide watch, I was woken up every half hour. This routine lasted two and a half weeks. The county psychologist was the only one with authority to release me from this icy eight-by-ten-foot prison cell.

Drug dealing is a federal offense. At a certain point, they hand you over to the feds. I had wondered why the US Marshals were involved. Now I knew. I was going to the big house.

There is a difference between the local police and the US Marshals. US Marshals know what illegal activity you have done. They already have enough evidence to place you in jail and get a conviction, and they will legally lay out the consequences of your decisions and actions before you. The local authorities had arrested me, but I knew that the federal authorities had gathered enough evidence to incriminate me.

God was overseeing all of my circumstances. (See Romans 8:28.) If I had been in the jail's area called general population, the other dealers and users who were arrested could have tagged me as a snitch or informer. And that accusation would not have been good for my health. Drug dealers, at any level, dislike to be snitched on, and I had not done that. I keep secrets very well. But they would have thought otherwise.

I didn't realize *my addiction had twisted me*, always looking for a way out, a fix, getting high, trying to dull the hurt. In jail or prison, the opportunity to score is mostly out of the question. I say *mostly* because, if you connect with certain prisoners, you can get things. However, the cost, not necessarily in dollars, is very high. So in getting high, you have to participate in low things. In federal prison, I chose to not reach out for any kind of contraband. All I wanted to do was keep to myself. That was something I could succeed at, much to my detriment.

Going to federal prison takes away every freedom you are accustomed to, and many you take for granted. You eat, go to bed, and take part in counseling when they say to. When you have open time, you need to decide where you want to be: in your cell, with the general population, at the library, or waiting in line for the phone. You can move to another module every forty-five minutes, but after that, the prison guards lock the doors, and you aren't able to change your location. You also have to wait in long, slow-moving lines for your prescription drugs to be dispensed.

The daily routine was to get up, maybe go to what they called breakfast, and then attend a session (if required or scheduled). Then it was time for lunch (high in carbohydrates), back to your cell, and rest or sleep (I did a lot of that). Gain weight, go to dinner, and back to your cell and your roomie, as your cellmate is called. Then the lights were turned off. And the whole routine would be repeated the next day.

Privacy was only a word. My cell was the standard cell, eight feet by ten feet. I had a bunk bed, a small writing table, a toilet (no wall around the commode), and a locker for the few things I could possess. Of course, bars were my wall to the hall, and guards would walk by. Whatever I was doing, they saw. I am sure the guards saw things that could not be unseen. That is prison life. The phrase *doing time* is exactly that, and time feels like it is at a standstill. The second hand on a clock becomes the hour hand and so on. In the first few days I realized I was a ward of the United States: I understood the meaning and absorbed the feeling of time standing still. My life, as I used to know it, was over.

I am writing this because I don't want or wish prison for anyone. You bury your true self deep within your soul. After your release, you can try to retrieve who you were before, but doing time leaves an emotional tattoo that never fades: a reminder of when you let "stupid" off the leash.

Dad's Story

I said, "Good night, I love you." I hung up the phone and rested, knowing my daughter was OK and going to bed. The evening was over. Barb and I were on our way from the tip of Texas to Spokane, Washington, to help a former daughter-in-law. We were staying in Las Vegas for the night. It had been a long day of traveling in our thirty-foot RV. We camped in one of the many RV parks in the city. *A perfect night*, was my thought. The weather was warm and sultry. We had traveled safely, found a comfortable RV park, and had a positive conversation with Jennifer. All in the world was wonderful as I drifted off to sleep, yet something in my subconscious was nagging at me. It was like an itch I couldn't quite scratch, and when I tried to, the itch didn't go away. I could not place what the problem was. Yet I slept, and the night was restful. Looking back, I can see that God gave us a sound night to refresh us because that next morning we found out what had gone on during the night.

The ringing of the cell phone interrupted our breakfast time. The number was one I didn't recognize, and I wondered if I should let the call go to voicemail or deny the call. Something in my soul said I needed to take the call. I picked up the call. It was Jennifer. Even before I could say hello, I heard, "I have been arrested and I am in jail." Time stopped. I could tell from her voice that this was reality, plus I knew she would not kid about being arrested and in jail. She told me the circumstances of what had happened.

Barb was looking at me with a concerned, puzzled look. I placed the phone on speaker, and Jennifer continued to share the midnight horror that had happened. Emotions from all three of us flew off the shelf like paper in a hurricane. We shared harsh words and confronted the fear we had never talked about that was now a reality. Jennifer was in jail and this was her one phone call. I was thankful she called me. But what could I do as a father? The reality of the situation hit both of us like an emotional tsunami. We were drowning

Going to Prison

in the fact that our youngest child was in jail and there was nothing we could do to erase or fix the situation.

The authorities disconnected the call; yelling at each other will do that. No goodbyes were said. I recall saying I loved her, but I don't think she heard, as she was an emotional mess. Barb and I sat in the confined space of our RV. Suddenly, the small square footage closed in on us. We needed distance from the reality of what we had heard and what was next for all of us.

Tears of sorrow clouded my eyes. My little daughter, my baby girl, was in jail on serious drug charges. The solution and situation were out of our hands. As missionaries, our funds were limited, and I felt I should follow the leading of our Lord in seeking a solution. Barb and I prayed for Jennifer's safety, and we asked for a legal miracle where she would be released and the charges would be dropped, if that was God's will.

We asked ourselves, *Should we turn around, go to Midland, Texas, and see what we can do? Will that help Jennifer? What is going to happen? When is the arraignment? Can we plead, speak on her behalf?* We didn't know what to do, if anything. We had never been down this path.

The conclusion we arrived at was, we could do nothing to lessen the trauma or the pending charges. The more we listened to the voice in our souls, the more we realized we were helpless. She was in the system, and the system would grind her out with a trial, sentencing, and prison time. All we could do was pray. The situation was not ours to solve, only to trust God.

By praying, we saw we were to continue with our travel plans. Each of us was in our silent world. Barb and I hardly spoke as the miles rolled under the tires of our RV. When we spoke, it was about some safe subject: where we would stop, the weather, anything but Jennifer's situation. I was in denial. Barb clearly saw the situation for what it was. Jennifer was in jail, charges pending, the future uncertain. My heart was silently crying for my daughter.

How deafening emotional silence is when the reality of trauma comes to roost in the family nest. There is no comfort in daily routine. Food tastes like cardboard mixed with sawdust. Moving in an emotional vacuum, you cannot recognize God's earthly beauty. Nothing looks beautiful or makes sense. You just try to breathe, and that is also difficult.

We know God is in control, His plan is in place. We must trust where He will lead us and how He will use the circumstance to His glory. But that is difficult because we want to solve the issue, slay the dragon ourselves. This is the precise time we need to rely wholly on His grace and mercy. It is never easy to let go and let God. However, we should look to His everlasting, loving light in the darkest of hours because that's where we'll find hope. His love, grace, and mercy will be available for our fractured heart to find rest in. Jeremiah says, "Call to me and I will answer you and tell you great and unsearchable things you do not know" (Jeremiah 33:3).

God was present, and that was clear in a call from the US Marshal's office. We had stopped for a rest. The phone rang, and now I answered any call. "Is this Robert Ruesch, the father of . . . Jennifer Lyn Ruesch?" the caller asked. I answered in the affirmative. The marshal introduced himself and asked a lot of questions about Jennifer and our relationship and a few about Jennifer's situation. He stated this was a background-information-gathering interview. After a while, he concluded the interview, but I told him I believed all things work out for the glory of God.

His response gave me hope and comfort. "Yes, Romans eight twenty-eight." With that, the call ended, and Jennifer's journey continued.

Do what you can, with what you have, where you are.
—*Theodore Roosevelt*

Chapter Nine

BEING IN PRISON

And we know that in all things, God works for the good of those who love him, who have been called according to his purpose.
—Romans 8:28

I listened when I was in court as the judge sentenced me to prison. I didn't understand, because I didn't think I would be sentenced to a correctional institution. There was no way I could have fathomed that I would be incarcerated at a federal prison. I thought that all of this must be a mistake. After all, I was a law-abiding citizen. The judge sentenced me to three years at a federal medical facility in Texas. As he read my sentence, I was in shock. This was never supposed to happen to me. My knees felt like rubber. I was a good girl who didn't get into trouble. My life philosophy was, try to get along with everyone and please everyone all the time. Sure, I did "a little" drugs, or so I thought. Being caught with drug dealers, I got the same legal treatment as they did. However, I found out later that my sentence was less than theirs, as I had not been present at the time of the purchase of the drugs. At least that was one "better" decision. Going along for the ride was simply completely stupid.

I barely heard my sentence. But, after I heard my legal future, the court bailiff immediately led me out of the courtroom. My wrists were handcuffed to a belt around my waist.

And my ankles were shackled. You will never know how emotionally devastating that makes you feel until you feel the cold metal and hear the clicking of the handcuffs, being restrained with "metal bracelets" and "ankle ware." I shuffled instead of walked. This was an experience not to be cherished. I was now a ward of the federal government, and all my needs would or would not be taken care of by the system.

What I wore to court was all I had. I would not be going back to pack a bag, and I could not have a travel bag with me. If I had thought ahead (and I did not), I would have donned extra underwear. What I had was all I had. I dealt with that reality immediately.

I was tethered to other women who had been sentenced, but there was no social interaction or conversation as we waited for the prison bus, which unceremoniously picked us up to take us to . . . we didn't really know where we were going. Looking out the window of the prison bus confirmed I was behind bars, as the windows were sealed and there was a metal lattice covering to look through.

Not a lot of smiles or any from now on. I was void of any positive emotion; I was now a ward of the US Government, and time was now my enemy.

There are certain sounds that continue to communicate to you that you are in prison. The noise never stops, even through the night. The metal clanging of cell doors, the squeaking of certain guards' shoes, the clicking sound of handcuffs being placed on you or someone else. Then there are the angry words between people. Nothing is positive about doing time.

When I arrived at Federal Medical Center, Carswell (FMC) in Fort Worth, Texas, I made a decision that I would not talk to anyone. I would keep to myself, do what I needed to do. I would keep my head down, make minimal eye contact. My plan was to sleep most of the day away, go to group sessions as

I was supposed to do, and not confront anyone on anything. I would do my time, get out, and move on.

That isn't the way it works in prison. There are the alpha people: they want to control you and everyone else and will call you out anytime they feel like bullying and berating you. They are action-oriented and have a way of telling you how you will respond to their gang's needs and requirements. It is common knowledge that crossing any of them is not advisable. Just do the math. You are on your own, and they are many.

Of course, that is against policy, but there is a lot that happens in a prison that isn't supposed to take place. I guess this is one reason the Admission and Orientation Handbook is fifty-seven pages of information. "The Admission and Orientation (A&O) Program and Handbook is developed to provide inmates new to the institution information regarding your rights and responsibilities as an inmate and the institution's disciplinary process, as well as programs available to you while incarcerated at this facility."

Federal Medical Center, Carswell, which was once a hospital, is where inmates with medical problems go. There are four floors, with each floor housing inmates with some medical issue. I got assigned a room on the fourth floor. There was no elevator. And with MS, stairs can be a challenge. My cellblock was 2 North with no room number. I had a bunkie, as the term goes. I tolerated my bunkie, as there was no privacy. Just a concrete cell with three walls, and the fourth space was open to the common area. There was a window looking to the outside, which had bars, of course. The room was stark, with no personality. It was about eight-by-ten feet, with two bunk beds, four small lockers, a small table, and a place to keep whatever stuff was mine. Forget about being alone: that was impossible.

The walls and floor were concrete, which radiated a frigid atmosphere supported by the steely chilling stare of my roomie. I walked in, holding all my possessions, and there I was, with no choice but to make the best of the situation, whatever that might be. Shana, one of my cellmates, was a hustler. She was out for herself and no one else. Shana was a large woman who knew her way about the system and prison. I felt fortunate to be assigned to her space, as she looked after me and had my back. Shana also watched her own back. She was that dominant. Her authority on the cellblock made me feel safer than the other inmates felt.

Shana and I spent three weeks together before they transferred me into the drug rehab program, Residential Drug Abuse Program (RDAP). I chose not to take part in sharing or offering any opinions. Looking back at that decision, I can see that did not help me address my situation. Of course, I didn't think I had a problem, and if I did, I could quit at the snap of a finger. Yeah, right, that is never the case, but addicts of any kind believe that lie as the truth.

What kept me in the RDAP was that I was in a better room and had a bottom bunk. In Shana's room I was on the top bunk, which was a challenge for me to climb up on to rest. The room was a repurposed hospital room, and I had three other roomies. The atmosphere was not as stressful or as tense as being in the general population. RDAP was safer, and I didn't have to watch my back as much. Still, I kept my head on a continual swivel. Again, my plan was to continue to keep to myself, not saying anything in group or individual sessions. I was NOT an addict, and I didn't need to be there, or so I continued to think.

Instead of joining in any of the sessions meant to help me, I stared blankly and remained silent. Being a human zombie was to be a prison life pattern for me. I didn't care a whit for who or what I was. Well, that is not exactly true. My strong desire was to be out of the rebar hotel, as I had named it. I wanted to be doing drugs. I had a small sliver of self-respect, but prison does interesting things to you. Your self-respect goes out the barred window. Everyone is wearing the same color, prison brown. You stand in lines waiting for doors to open, then hear the metallic slamming of them being shut and locked either in front of or behind you.

Every step you take, you are watching and listening to sounds around you. You are in a consistent state of hyper-awareness. Will someone confront, attack, or threaten you? You never know what will happen. What you know is that something will eventually happen to someone somewhere, and you could get in the middle of the altercation. The other realization is, you continue to hear, "I am innocent. I didn't do it. I got blamed. It was the other person." That continual deflection of reality gets old quick. You are cautious to ask the other prisoners what they are in for. Many will volunteer, others you would just rather not know.

Ink (tattoos) is a big thing in prison. There is an unwritten rule: the more tats, the greater the sentence. You are walking among thieves, grifters, sociopaths, liars, and murderers (who also didn't do it). Of course, there are the bullies who will take what they want of yours, so you keep your few possessions close at hand and secured. You have little, so what you have is precious to you. There is a barter process in place. Some cellmates may have something you can use and you may have an item they need. Let the negotiations begin.

When a person has done their time, they can leave with what they have. Many times, those who leave sell or give away certain cherished items like radios, toiletry items, shoes, and other necessary items. When a person departs, there is a realignment of the prison pecking order, as a new resident will replace that person, but where will the new inmate fit in the hierarchy of order?

Prison guards are another topic. Some inmates call them "bulls," and that term can certainty fit many of them. I suppose, in some ways, they are as much in prison as you are. But they go home at night. Many of the guards in the prison system have experienced decades of anger, hurt, and manipulation, which can make them appear uncaring. Many of the guards possess compassion, but showing it is a sign of weakness. Compassion can be a fatal trait for them. They have to be tough but understanding. Many guards will carry on a conversation with you, however stilted. After all, you are under their authority, and they can make your time miserable or easy but never comfortable.

One of the first guards I encountered in the first prison I was in purposely broke my glasses with no regrets. She was simply mean. Over time, I learned which guards to avoid, which ones I could talk to, and which ones to not even make eye contact with. I also learned to do this with the inmates in my cellblock, if I wanted to avoid bruises.

I am not saying all of this to garner sympathy. But prison is prison. You are there because you did something against the law and you are paying for that infraction. The sooner you understand the why of where you are, the better. Some guards and inmates will help you reach that revelation. And the sooner you realize you are not going anywhere, the better. Inmates and guards are excellent teachers, and class is always in session. Either you understand and learn, or you pay for the consequences of your attitude with body bruises. This is not a place for the weak. You can become mean because it allows you to survive.

Have an attitude, get attitude. Push back, get thrown down. Sometimes physically, always emotionally. Mouth off, listen to the one-sided lesson and lecture. Do negative things, receive negative responses. Sometimes that means solitary confinement or being told to stay in your cell, all 150 square feet of it.

I pray you are taking what I am saying to heart. I pray you will listen to that still, quiet, thundering voice in your soul and discern what you are thinking of doing. Being on the "outside," you have rights. You can go where you want, when you want. In prison, that is not the case. Remember I said you have a commode in your cell? Well, you can go when you want . . . with everyone in your cellblock knowing what you are doing. That is about the only thing you can do when you want.

The best thing you will finally hear is that you are being released. You have counted the days, the hours, and finally the minutes. You wait, and when that moment arrives, you walk out to a halfway house. It is time to be reintroduced back into society. In my case, I looked for old "friends," and that got me another opportunity I didn't want.

When everything seems to be going against you, remember that the airplane takes off against the wind, not with it.
—Henry Ford

Chapter Ten

PSYCHOLOGICAL DIAGNOSIS

But now, this is what the Lord says—
he who created you, Jacob,
he who formed you, Israel:
"Do not fear, for I have redeemed you;
I have summoned you by name; you are mine."
—Isaiah 43:1

When you are reassigned to another federal facility, several courses of travel are available to you. If you are moving a small distance, a police cruiser will transport you. If you are going a little further, you will be treated to a trip on the prison bus, complete with shackles, handcuffs, and gender segregation. There will be the bars on the windows. Some buses have a chain-link fence inside to protect the driver and the guard; some buses even have cages.

However, if your destination is much farther across the USA, you are transported on Con Air, a private airline for the US federal prison system. Same thing goes here: all the hardware a girl could ever want to wear! You will be in handcuffs and shackles and chained to the persons in front and back of you. You shuffle in and are locked in, and there is minimal talking or socializing.

Here is the killer: you better relieve yourself before the flight because it almost takes an act of Congress to get the air guards to release you for the "necessary room," in which there is no privacy. But you already knew that. Believe me, this necessary experience on Con Air is something you never forget.

Men are loaded on first. Women are seated in the airplane's forward section. There is no first, business, or regular class. By the way, there are no refreshments served. You are told not to have eye contact with any other person. Glancing at them can cause some sort of disciplinary action for you and the person you looked at.

Arriving in California for my diagnosis was a pleasant change from the federal prison I was at in Oklahoma City. They assigned me to the Metropolitan Detention Center in Los Angeles. This building is several stories tall and as cold as a prison should be, but the medical and psychological staff were pleasant to work with.

My cell, like most prison cells, was void of most creature comforts. There was the usual bunk bed, a metal sink, a toilet, and two lockers for whatever possessions I had. And again, that was not much. There was a window through which I could look out and see the city. I enjoyed looking out at night, as the lights twinkled, and I could occasionally hear traffic sounds of people who were free to go where they wanted, which was not me. I thought a lot about the circumstantial choices that had brought me there. I missed the laughter of freedom especially at night when I would wish I could just go for an evening walk. I was alone with my thoughts, which made the sorrow of being locked up much more realistic because I could hear the sounds of freedom.

The whole prison thing was on me. It was because of my decision. I knew that, sitting in my prison cell, staring at the off-white concrete walls. I was alone, even with a roommate. Alone, with a solid window that was locked. Bars on the door, one light in a cold and unfriendly room with concrete walls. They say Los Angeles is the city of angels. I was in what they called the city of angels, but there were no angels in this building. Just 620 inmates waiting each day for another day of the same.

As always, there was the daily routine. I was required to be up at 5 AM for breakfast, which was served in the common area, tray style, with a twist of prison spice thrown in for good measure. What they gave me was what I ate. If I didn't want the food, I didn't eat. No exceptions. We ate all our meals in the common area, right next to the gym equipment. We cleaned up our trays and went about the day. At 10, we were secure (a nice way to say locked) in our cells until the noon meal, again tray style. Then we had "free" time until another secure time in our cells at 3:30. They served dinner at 5:30 and then locked us in our cells for the night's sleep at 10 PM. This was the forever routine each day. Nothing changed. I had to figure out a way to know what day it was.

Reading was my go-to escape, but it was not easy to read because of the side effects I was prescribed. I was on drugs for bipolar, depression, diabetes, and blood pressure. The medicine changed my ability to read books after the dosages were adjusted to what the doctors thought they needed to be. I played cards to pass the time. For entertainment, some of the girls would talk to the male inmates through the vent system. I didn't see any value in this activity. Who would what to pursue a relationship that way?

Finally, after a few weeks of waiting, the evaluations began. I was doing time, so I had lots of time to think about what I would say, what I would not say. I was a sly one, except the staff had seen it all, so as opaque as I thought I was, to them I was transparent. My evaluations were one-on-ones and scheduled for an hour each week, but in reality, every two weeks seemed like the average. Sometimes the session would last two hours. The session length depended on the attitude of the counselor, or maybe it was the attitude I projected. I was always nervous when doing my cognitive evaluation sessions. The first time I met my counselor I was shaking so much I had to hide my hands. I went through cognitive testing, math questions, and personality questions—everything to get into my well-protected brain to figure out who I was.

When the sessions were over, I thought, *That was it?* I didn't think I was any better than when I went in. There was homework I had to do to evaluate myself. I didn't do the required homework, as that would require an effort on my part. Mad, angry, despondent, and pissed off—that was my attitude. I did not deserve to be here, or so I thought. I would cast that attitude to all three of my counselors. I transcended all of this psychological nonsense, and I felt exempt from any rules or regulations. After all, I'd had an argument with the sentencing judge about going here. (Note to self and everyone: do not argue with a judge, you will never win.)

I realized while reading my twenty-seven-page single-spaced psychological profile that the staff had been observing me all the time. I guess that was what the security cameras were for. As in any prison, I was never alone, but I was in mental solitude all the time. Everyone had to look out for themselves. I was a small fish swimming in an ocean of hungry sharks.

To survive, I made alliances. Other inmates thought I was lucky, but I didn't believe in luck. I believed in God's protection, and He gave me roomies who were high on the scale of scary to other inmates. They carried the word not to mess with, talk to, or confront me, as there would be ramifications and consequences that could, well, would, not be comfortable for an inmate's health. There were several times I saw what they meant when an inmate crossed them. Even with cameras,

Psychological Diagnosis

things happened. I understand God's protection more now, like Daniel in the lion's den or Shadrach, Meshach, and Abednego in the fiery furnace. God was with me, even when I didn't know it or when I doubted His presence.

Every prison situation I was in, I had the protection of the gang that was in control of the cellblock. Even in Los Angeles I was the roomie of the leader of the block we were in. That was not by chance but by God.

When I was first jailed, in Midland, I spent over three weeks in solitary confinement on suicide prevention.

When you are in solitary and on suicide watch, you don't have a mattress or pillow. Just a hard cot bolted to the wall to sleep on. You are wearing what they call a "turtle suit." This garment, an anti-suicide smock, or suicide gown, is a tear-resistant single-piece outer garment. Inmates on suicide watch are placed in this garment. (It looks like something Fred Flintstone would wear.) It prevents the incarcerated, or otherwise detained, individual from forming a noose with the garment to commit suicide with. I had a blanket, no pillow.

Sleep does not come easy, as the guards are checking on you every hour, all day and all night long, to see if you are among the living. You respond to the guards calling you. Lights on, smiles everywhere. You never know who really "cares" until you cut yourself to create another form of hurt and pain.

This suicide solitary time was sufficient for all the other offenders who were arrested that same night to be processed out. Many were moved to federal facilities. I was moved to a federal facility in Oklahoma City. My roomie was the former roomie of the Women's Director of Teen Challenge, where I had been for over a year and a half! And when I came back from the "vacation" in Los Angeles, guess who I bunked with? You guessed it, the same person. You cannot out give God's provision and protection. I believe all of us travel through life oblivious to the many dark dangers that are around us.

Psychological evaluation under the federal government's care introduced a new reality. I was forced to look at who I was and who the counselors diagnosed me to be. So here goes, this is a broad description of who they and I think I might be.

One report I took was called "International Personality Item Pool - Neuroticism, Extraversion, and Openness" or IPIP-NEO for short. This test was accepted as the standard test of a person's personality traits. A decade ago, when the tests were administered to me, much of the test results were accurate. Yet God takes you and molds you if you allow His presence in your life. In prison, I did not want Him to heal me. I thought I could heal myself. Wrong.

The IPIP-NEO test looks at five areas of who you are: extraversion, agreeableness, conscientiousness, neuroticism, and openness to experience. But there is another evaluation that is more extensive (remember the twenty-seven pages of "me"?). I won't dwell on the results here too much and only share the general results. So here goes.

Extraversion states I was introverted, reserved, and quiet. I enjoyed solitude and solitary activities. My social structure was with a few friends. True enough at that time in my life.

Agreeableness: I was average, I had some concern for others' needs, and I was reluctant to sacrifice myself for others. (Well then, how did I end up with the nefarious friends I had? I think we know the answer to that.)

Conscientiousness - Here was an extremely low score. I would live for the moment. I would do what felt good. My work was careless and disorganized. (Welcome to the world of an addict. No excuses, just reality.)

Neuroticism: Well, finally a high score! I could be easily upset, even by the normal demands of daily living. I had over-the-top anxiety and immoderation (the quality of being excessive and lacking in restraint, overindulgence). Of course, anger is part of these diagnoses along with depression.

Openness to Experience: I scored low here too. I admit I still like to think in plain and simple terms. Life was not fun or happy for me then. I still like to keep it simple, comfortable, but following God's will.

Now I see and understand Ephesians 4:32: "And be kind to one another, tenderhearted, forgiving one another, even as God in Christ forgave you" (NKJV). I was kind to others only to get them to like me. I was tenderhearted if it meant I could get something from someone. *Forgiving* was not in my emotional vocabulary. You messed with me, I got even.

Today I reflect on where any of us would be in the realm of eternity if God didn't forgive. I now see His faithfulness, His love, His grace, and His mercy. Thank God!

To know God can clean up any mess, including mine, is a comfort to me today.

The federal system continued to observe, test, and interview me, and that resulted in a comprehensive deep dive into where I was in my life. I do not intend to bore you with more psychobabble, but it is important to understand just how gutter low I was at that time in 2014.

In many of my sessions, I told the counselor that "I was in a pit of despair." I said, "All I want to do is sleep." And that I did, which led to a diagnosis of bipolar disorder. So I was medicated. Once again, I got to swallow pills and more pills. I was on an addict's pill parade of five neurological drugs.

Here is what was said about where I was in life: "Ms. Ruesch is currently suffering from emotional or mental symptoms with the intensity and duration necessary to meet the DSM-5 (Diagnostic and Statistical Manual of Mental Disorders, Fifth Addition) for Major Depressive Disorder."

The diagnosis further states, "There is borderline Personality Disorder, Severe Alcohol Disorder, Recurrent, Moderate Methamphetamine Use Disorder."

What a mess, but our God cleans up messes. All I had to do was ask Him for His help. I was not ready to do that. Seeking His help would come years, well, a decade later. Addicts don't learn easily, and that is part of the reason for so many addict deaths.

The prognosis stated my diagnosis of major depressive disorder was fair. My personality disorder was "guarded" according to this exhaustive report. It was stated that I could have a positive future if I could abstain from substance abuse. That, we know, was the monkey on my back. God was the only deity that could release me from my addictions. I am alive today because of God's grace and mercy. Because I am one of His chosen, I will serve Him until my last breath on earth.

Read and memorize the following verses. Sear them upon your heart. Live them each day. They are the true Word of God and will continue to sustain you and give you hope to conquer the demons that torment you. Why be tormented when you can be set free?

Forget the former things; do not dwell on the past.
—Isaiah 43:18

And we all, who with unveiled faces contemplate the Lord's glory, are being transformed into his image with ever-increasing glory, which comes from the Lord, who is the Spirit.
—2 Corinthians 3:18

Therefore, if anyone is in Christ, the new creation has come: The old has gone, the new is here.
—2 Corinthians 5:17

Psychological Diagnosis

Believe.

The strongest action for a woman is to love herself, be herself and shine amongst those who never believed she could.
—Unknown

Chapter Eleven

RE-OFFENDED

WELCOME BACK

*I am more than a conqueror in all things,
for nothing can separate me from God's love!*
—Romans 8:37, 39 (author's paraphrase)

November 2016

Some things you just have to learn more than once. With going to prison, that was the case for me. I re-offended and became the guest of the federal government a second time. Sometimes it is difficult to fix stupid, and in my case, I let stupid off its leash, and I did it again!

Going to prison is not a vacation, and if you believe going back to the big house the second time is easier, it is not; it is more of a defeat. You have failed again.

When you are an addict, illegal substance abuse catches you in an ever-tight net. I tested positive for cocaine use. I did not do cocaine, and how my test came back positive for cocaine is a mystery to me. My probation officer was not pleased that I did not pass clean. Boom, crash, done. I was on my way back to the place where I said I would never return: prison. Silly me, dumb, bad, weak, sad, and mad Jennifer.

Because of drinking and using drugs (Adderall), the judge threw the law book at me. I was charged with everything he could legally think of. I recall him saying that I was an idiot and didn't know what I was doing. He also made the remark that I was weak, susceptible to other people's direction and influence. All of that was true.

My offense resulted in thirty-six months in prison. I was also sentenced to three months at a federal rehab facility. And, of course, an ankle monitor for twelve months.

Here is what ChatGPT says about my new again home:

FMC Carswell is a federal medical center in Fort Worth, Texas, primarily designated for female inmates. The facility focuses on providing medical and mental health services to incarcerated women. Inmates with various needs receive specialized medical care at the facility. FMC Carswell aims to maintain a secure environment, addressing the unique health care requirements of its population. The facility is crucial in the federal prison system, as it prioritizes rehabilitating and treating women offenders.

I returned to Carswell, where I had lived for over two and a half years—welcome "home." Carswell houses 990 women inmates who need medical treatment. This is the only federal facility to support treatment. I received admission to the hospital unit, which was a blessing, as the unit was better than the general population area of the facility.

Coming back was not the family reunion I wanted to experience. I kept to myself. If there was a required meeting, I would go, but I checked out and listened to my heartbeat, not the counselor. (Just like last time.) Because of me not taking part, I was constantly called out by the prison counselor and some of the inmates. I didn't care; being in that cold, hard, mean place was not my idea. All I wanted to do was do my time, get out, and probably get high.

When you are in this type of institution, you are still doing time. In a medical facility, you stand in line for hours at a time for your medications, which brings a whole new meaning to *doing time*. By the time you are at the front of the line, you are bored and worn out. Standing in line is not a social event: you avoid making eye contact and only exchange brief apologies (if you dare) when you accidentally collide with the person in front of or behind you.

Even if there are no bars on the windows and the public space is open, you have already constructed bars around yourself. Your bunkie might or might not be on your side. God protected me with a person who was one of the alpha females of the prison. She protected me from harm, for which I am forever grateful.

I am not saying there were not some positive times, but they were few. Holidays were special, with a better meal and some relaxing of the rules. Yet spending Thanksgiving, Christmas, and your birthday with 990 inmates who couldn't care less how lonely and sad you are feeling, well, you get the picture. Besides having the privilege of standing forever in lines for medications, meetings, and meals, I invested my time in reading. I could escape into my personal world. Although I'm unsure of the exact number of books I read, I distinctly recall devouring the entire Stephanie Plum series by Janet Evanovich. I believe I read twenty-six of the thirty books. Reading and sleeping, eating, and going to wait in line was my preferred social schedule.

I believe I was more than protected by my Lord and Savior. Prison is a cauldron of negative emotion, and many times physical responses erupt between two or more inmates. There is a consistent battle among the inmates to be the group (gang) alpha boss. Creating fear and proving that your actions back up the anger and negative emotion you have shown are essential to establishing yourself in this position. As I have previously mentioned, my bunkie was that alpha person and put the word out that I was not to be involved in any challenge. I believe she felt I should not be there. (You see, every person in prison is innocent.) In her case, I was a "good person" who got a bad rap. She had received a five-year sentence after being found guilty of bank robbery. Her nickname was Red because of her flaming red hair. Sometimes I feel God gave some women red hair as a warning sign for others to be aware of them and their personality.

The courts released me at the appointed time, but my halfway house (Alpha House) would not be available for a month to six weeks, which would mean I would be in a state or county jail facility. I was going back to Midland, Texas, which would place me in the Ector County Correctional Center. That was where I had started my jail journey. I felt that was not a safe place for me, even after several years. One thing to remember, criminals have a long memory, and payback for something you might have done stays "on the books."

I was unaware of what was going on in the background, but my dad had a conversation with my parole officer. He complained about the location of my temporary incarceration. The parole officer was also not comfortable with Ector County. There was a more than better chance some of the original offenders from years back could be there. That could mean emotional and/or physical harm for me as a perceived informant. Snitches are not very popular with inmates. (Remember, I said criminals never forget.)

My dad talked to Teen Challenge in Midland. They agreed to allow me to stay on their property until a space opened up for me in the halfway house in San Antonio. Again, God directed many facets of my transfer, as this residence was an unusual place for someone who was waiting for their opening at the halfway house to stay. This had never happened in the past. I believe God, once again, like with my bunkie in Carswell, assured my safety. Not necessarily my comfort, but my safety.

After six weeks at TC, I was transferred to Alpha House for three months to reintegrate back into society. I tried as hard as I could to hurt myself or find a drink or drug supplier. I was always looking for ways to dull the hurt. Yet God was there for my safety, from myself and sometimes others.

Alpha House was a warm, welcome change from Carswell Prison. There was limited freedom with a schedule, rules, and responsibilities. My time there went by quickly. I stayed within the lines and did what I was told, but I was always looking for a fix and finding none. Not being able to score helped me lower my craving for something, anything. Yet the craving would return when I moved to my new home, Oxford House.

At Oxford House, I was expected to get a job, take on chores, and take part in weekly meetings. I had my own room. The first night I was there, I took a shower, forgetting to place the shower curtain in the tub. "Cleanup on the second-floor bathroom." Talk about embarrassing and making a negative impression. What I learned was that the other residents were not accusatory or angry. I think they believed I was unbalanced, and they were right. My longing for some illegal drug was becoming a consistent craving. That is always an issue with addicts. Give them a few yards of freedom, and they

Re-offended

will go miles in the wrong direction. I was on my downfall journey once again.

I got a job at one of those discount dollar stores stocking shelves, running the cash register, and whatever else needed to be done. Watching people walk out without paying for items, I thought, W*hy don't they get caught like I did?* After a few months, they offered me an assistant manager position. Not really more money, yet doing the same thing, only with a set of keys.

One day, I came to work and noticed there was a hole in the store's outside wall. Someone had really wanted something, and I was reluctant to find out what was going on in the store. The manager said to open anyway, nice for employee safety. I feel that sped up my craving for numbing the hurt. If the manager didn't care about me going into a store where someone could have been, what was I to the company?

I was bored and registered on a dating website. That was when I met Minus One. (That was the nickname my dad give this guy. *Insignificant Other* was more of a challenge to say. Dad rarely used his name, and we won't use his name in this book.) We planned a date to meet. I was impressed as he pulled up in an expensive car. I opened the door (no, he didn't do the gentlemanly thing and come around to open the door for me). When I opened the door, I could smell that the vehicle reeked of marijuana. I said, "You smoke weed." It was not a question but a statement. I was on federal probation, and being in this situation would cancel my probation. I told him he could not smoke around me. That didn't last but a few days. Being desperate for a boyfriend, I got in the car anyway.

That incident triggered me, and I knew at that moment, buckling my seatbelt, I didn't want to be sober. I wanted something, and I knew just how to make my addictive desire happen. I found out later that Minus One had connections.

The store I worked at sold compressed air (air duster for cleaning electronics), and that was going to be my fix. It is called "huffing." Compressed air doesn't show up in drug tests, but it should. I was unsuccessful in scoring anything on the street, so I turned to something off the shelf. Well, if others took things and management had the same low opinion of me that I already had of myself, why not take a can or two and huff away? It seemed like an excellent idea.

Inhaling air duster can have serious health consequences. The product contains various chemicals such as difluoroethane. When inhaled, the chemicals can displace oxygen in the lungs, leading to oxygen deprivation. Short-term effects include dizziness, lightheadedness, and hallucinations. Long-term exposure can cause damage to the central nervous system and vital organs. People have died from huffing.

Inhaling air duster can also lead to a sudden drop in blood pressure, heart palpitations, and loss of consciousness. The risks extend beyond the immediate effects, as repeated inhalation can cause addiction and irreversible damage to the respiratory and cardiovascular systems. Immediate medical attention is crucial when you do this deed to your body. So I huffed.

I passed out at work. The manager wanted to know what happened. I said I was tired and didn't need any medical treatment. The fire department paramedics were called anyway and released me after a brief field exam. The store let me go from the rest of my shift since it was almost over. (How does a drug-compromised person work effectively at all?)

Walking home is something I don't fully recall, but I had my hidden can of duster and would huff again when I was in my room. That was my plan. On the way home, I stumbled and fell two times from what I was told. Once home, I passed out again and had a minor seizure. The paramedics were again called; the same ones showed up and saw the same symptoms as before. However, this time, they realized what I had done. I often wonder if the aerosol can was where the medics could see it.

The staff and paramedics reported my behavior to the head of Oxford House. The rules at Oxford House were brutally clear. If you used, you had fifteen minutes to pack and get out. I found myself and my belongings on the front porch and was told to get out and leave. I could not enter this program again; those were their rules, and I had broken them.

I called my probation officer, stating that I was moving in with my "boyfriend." Telling my PO my new address was required for my probation. Probation officers have heard and seen it all. She knew what I had done, as I was honest with her, although I would have liked to have given some lame reason for the move. I believe she suspected something more than just a drug-related incident had happened. My next required drug test was clean, or that would have been my third offense. That would have meant being back in prison with no chance of parole. (Dodged that legal bullet, but I still didn't learn.)

Minus One came and got me. Little did I know how the decision to huff and then call him would affect my life for the next six years. From the moment I smelled marijuana in his car on our first date, I should have known he was more than terrible news. But addicts don't recognize, or refuse to see, danger signs. After all, we are bulletproof, or so we are duped into thinking.

The first thing he did in moving my stuff was give my television to his mother. That should have been a warning, but I didn't see it, or I ignored it, probably both. I felt emotionally devastated when they kicked me out of the program. I was doing so well, and going with him seemed like my only option. That was when he started placing his narcissistic enticements in me. I was hooked, like a fish on a line. All he had to do now was reel me in. And that he did, because he was an expert in manipulation, deception, and deceit. Next chapter, same verse.

> *Our greatest glory is not in never falling,*
> *but in rising every time we fall.*
> *—Confucius*

Chapter Twelve

THE ADDICT AND THE NARCISSIST

*I am more than a conqueror in all things,
for nothing can separate me from God's love!*
—Romans 8:37, 39 (author's paraphrase)

True narcissists don't care about others' feelings. They also do not understand or comprehend the effect that their manipulative behavior has on other people.

Their talons are sharper than a surgeon's scalpel. They reel you in with wonderful words, kind love bombs, and endearing talk. You are hooked. Harpooned like a fish. All this before you see it. Then, most times, it is too late.

However, getting out of the toxic, negative relationship is, in some ways, incredibly easy. Easy to do, but difficult to execute. The narcissist will continue to hound you like a dog after their favorite bone to come back, to be a "positive" part of their life, which is a negative for you. They will bomb you with flowers, cards, and "I'm sorry." They will tell you anything to get you back and under their control again.

So let's go back to the beginning, the first mistake, when I saw the warning signs of danger.

I was lonely, and, as I said before, my picker is not good with male relationships. Over my lifetime of relationships, there was a breakup every time. They failed because of my choices. Having an addiction simply exacerbates the relationship issue. And I am an addict.

As you know, I was in a supportive and safe halfway house. I had a job as an assistant manager at a small convenience store. The money I was earning was not terrific, but I was surviving and was part of the management committee at the halfway house. Life was good. A private room, my own TV—things were going my way. Then the thought came to my mind that I needed a boyfriend. I complicated my lack of judgment by posting my profile on one of those lesser-known dating Internet sites. If you ever think of doing this, watch out. Make a different decision (or figure out something else). This was not the right site. I believe there are Christian dating websites out there, but I am also acquainted with people who found their true north on the platform I used. I soon found a person who did not possess a true north for me but was instead pointing only at himself.

As you remember, my dad named him "Minus One." When you are in a positive relationship, you have a significant other or a plus one. However, now in my life, he is in the past. I thank God for protecting me (again) for the six years I was with him. My dad has said that God has worked overtime to keep me protected and safe. I know it has been God because I fully admit I was not protecting myself. Welcome to addiction.

Like I said previously, our first date smelled of weed when I opened the door of his car; he didn't get out to open it for me (red flags number one and two). I was still on probation and had every reason to not get in the car at first breath. That could and would violate my probation. But I did. Closing the door of the car sealed my fate and put my life on a descending path of hurt, self-hate, personal doubt, and negative self-image.

The Addict and the Narcissist

In the beginning, he was kind, wonderful, and caring, to a fault (red flag number three). He swept me off my feet, and I landed firmly on my butt. He lived with his grandma and "took care of her," so he said. Guess who started taking care of her? You guessed it: me. I became the primary caregiver, not that I minded. I like to help, and I came to love his grandma. She was a gentle and caring eighty-year-old woman. However, she often got run over by the narcissistic freight train that was her grandson. Daily actually. Both of us got freight trained every day. That lifestyle became the new normal of my life.

Over time, these relationships spiral down. Being in a situation with a narcissistic person will make you doubt who you are every day. A narcissistic setting creates a continual flight, fight, and fear mode.

I found this definition of *narcissism* on the web: "Narcissism is extreme self-involvement to the degree that it makes a person ignore the needs of those around them. While everyone may show occasional narcissistic behavior, true narcissists frequently disregard others or their feelings. They also do not understand the effect that their behavior has on other people."[4]

Finally, I could see I was in a dangerous predicament and it would not get any better. So I did what I always do. I numbed the hurt by seeking any downer drug I could get my hands on and swallow.

Moving in with Minus One and his grandmother seemed like the only option I had. At least that was my thinking. I remember the TV I had purchased became his mom's a few miles away because there was no room in his grandmother's house (red flag number four). We trundled the rest of my belongings into a spare room, and I was, once again, in a prison. This time no bars on the windows, but they were on my soul.

A major red flag I missed was his age. He had never been married. How many men, forty years and counting, live with a grandma and have never been married? (Giant waving red flag.) When you are desperate and needy, you don't see the warning signs. Well, if you do, you ignore them. I sure did, and I paid a high price, almost with my life.

As I am writing this chapter, I am still traumatized by this relationship. It seems I cannot release myself from many things that happened. I continue to get nightmares, but through Christian counseling, the sleeping trauma is becoming less and less. I believe many counselors would say this is a form of post-traumatic stress disorder (PTSD), which soldiers and many paramilitary people experience.

Here is one of many examples I can give you about the trauma of living this type of life. Once, I thought it would be a friendly gesture to make a batch of lemon bars. He was always controlling my money, but I had enough to purchase the ingredients to make a wonderful batch of homemade lemon bars. Minus One bought lemon bar mix instead because he wanted that taste. I made a pan of lemon bars. As the bars baked, the house smelled like my childhood home. When I was a child, my dad and I baked together just once. That wonderful memory was on my mind as I pulled the pan out of the oven, perfectly baked to a scrumptious golden yellow. I believed Minus One would appreciate my effort for something sweet and tasty.

Guess what? He wanted round cookies, not bars, so they were never tasted. Minus One only liked cookies to be round. He lost his temper (actually, I believe he had never even located his temper). He took the pan and tossed them into the trash, yelling and hollering during the entire episode.

This is only one of thousands of examples of how a narcissist goes from zero to one hundred on the anger scale in a split second. You never know when the anger will come. All you know is, you are constantly walking on boiling water, and you will get burned almost every day. And you wonder why you stay.

The claws of a narcissistic person continue to hook you deeper and deeper. Welcome to another form of addiction and to codependency. I knew something would happen and he would blame me for it. Then the rodeo of unreason would begin. The accusations, yelling, unreal expectations, rule changes—he could accomplish all of this by yelling, screaming, running around flailing his arms, and looking for something to throw and break. He condemned me for anything and everything; it was an over-the-top emotional rodeo of unreason with unreal expectations and changing rules! Suddenly, he didn't like lemon cookies in any form.

Please don't assume I am looking for a pity party. Not so. I can see intellectually, but I am blind emotionally. I know I could have taken charge and closed out this relationship. It was time for this chapter of my life to end and for me to be me, the person God intended me to be. Yet I stayed. Low self-esteem created in me from the consistent badgering sucked my strength to leave and move on.

A narcissist will do and say all the right things to get you to accept that everything will be better. However, better will never be the case.

Here are some truths to consider:

1. Narcissists don't stay with partners they love the most. They stay with partners who love themselves the least.
2. Proverbs 9:8 says, "Do not rebuke mockers or they will hate you; rebuke the wise and they will love you." When you try to reason with this negative behavior, you will get nowhere because opinion, thought, and

logic do not matter to them. They know only their truth, whatever that is. Nothing but receiving Jesus will change this negative, overbearing behavior.

Here is a better way of thinking: avoid people who play the victim after they have disrespected you, bullied you, thrown negative criticism and false accusations at you, and made cruel, mean, and hurtful comments. They will not show any regard for your feelings. Matter of fact, they will treat you as damaged goods, unwanted matter.

Minus One accused me of using drugs all the time. Many times, this was correct. The emotional pressure was oppressive. Drugs are not the answer in any circumstance like this. Jesus is the answer. Know this and know it well.

Narcissistic people know EXACTLY what they are doing, and they are aware they are hurting you. They are not victims in any sense of the word. They choose their behaviors and are intentional in their actions against you. All this is manipulation to keep you off center, ever vigilant, scared, and worrying when the next mallet will fall. You know it is coming; it's just a matter of when.

A narcissist is a child trapped in time who is wandering around in an adult body. They are frozen in their childish moment, and they are needing you to validate them. You take the blame for their actions, and they continually say you are the one at fault. A narcissist's major goal is to get an angered reaction out of you. They will poke and prod you to the point of you losing your temper or doing something out of character. This is their way of not having to take any accountability or responsibility for their actions. They don't change. They spin it so that it looks like you are the problem, which you are not.

This person must be taken off the pedestal of authority that you have so unwillingly placed them on. It does no good to engage with them on any level. It is easier for them to "remember" things that never actually happened while forgetting about those things that did.

There are several things that need to happen for you to heal, to be released from this emotional quicksand that is pulling the personality and life out of you. One, you must stop explaining things to a narcissist. By not justifying any accused action, there is little or no argument, which brings me to number two. You can't argue. It takes two to fight. Remember what Jesus did. He remained quiet. Silence is deadly to a narcissist. Number three, if you are defending your actions or self, you might as well throw gasoline on the fire. You supply an emotional fuel for the person to burn hotter. And finally, when you try to explain something, well, that never happens, because the narcissist already knows that what they understand is the explanation. Your reasoning never counts in the eyes of this disorder.

Nothing is accomplished by talking with a narcissist. All talking does is create frustration for you and fuel for the other person. There is no winning an argument with a narcissist because narcissists possess an overdeveloped sense of entitlement. They will condition you to become obsessed with monitoring their mood and keeping them happy 24/7. If you don't, there will be repercussions. Most of the time, you cannot predict when the explosion will come. Yet the crisis, the explosion, the issue is coming, and it will involve you. That is your reality.

You cannot win with a narcissist. There is nothing you can do to correct this behavior yourself. Correction and change need to originate with them. Here is a list I find helpful about why you can't win:

1. The person is always looking to win the battle. You are looking for a positive resolution.
2. Narcissists firmly believe they are right and never, ever wrong. That means there is not any accountability, understanding, or validation. "My way or the highway" thinking.
3. Their goal is to dominate you at all costs to you. What you want, what makes you happy, is inconsequential, unnecessary, and unneeded to them.
4. What is important to them is all that matters. Your importance means nothing.
5. They believe they are perfect, which means everything is your or someone else's fault.
6. Because they believe the superiority of themselves, anything you bring to the conversation or argument means absolutely nothing.
7. The characteristics they display are not compatible with any emotional (and sometimes physical) intimacy. There is a disconnect that takes away their ability to engage in healthy relationships.

Narcissists isolate you from everyone who has been in your life. That allows them to control you because now there is nobody in your life. I realized that once I was isolated and dependent on this person, I was easier to control and abuse. I learned in this relationship that a narcissist cannot self-reflect. They cannot see anything that is incorrect about what they are doing. As previously mentioned, everything is your fault. Every argument (started by them) is caused by you. Why? Because, to them, there is not a problem with any of their actions until there is a reaction from you to them. They fully believe you are the problem and they are the victim.

There were too many times to count when I found myself abandoned in public places because of his decision to control me. He would drive off, leaving me on the side of the road or in a parking lot. I would be left with no identification, money, and, many times, no way to call for help. Of course, he would come back within fifteen minutes to half an hour. He would act as if the situation was completely my fault. The next day, the "love bombs" would start coming. He sometimes apologized for his actions, but was it really an apology or just a way to further control me? There would be stuffed animals, flowers, and chocolate, and he would let me see that these items cost a lot of money. That was a guilt bomb. I didn't ask, and I really didn't want any of this stuff. However, if I refused the love bombs, or didn't show a positive response to the items, BOOM! Another incident.

Self-doubt was my continual feeling while being in this negative relationship for over six years. I was afraid of what would happen when the situation became too difficult for me to handle emotionally. As I mentioned before, an addict is an addict. We are wired with a hair trigger, and that can send us spiraling down, seeking a fix. Remember, a narcissist is like a snake that only sheds their skin to become a bigger snake.

Minus One promised me he would take me to see my son in Florida. I was anxious, as I had not seen him in several years. Maybe Minus One had maliciously changed and shed his narcissistic personality. We traveled from Texas to Florida to see my son. I loved seeing and being with Kaleb. But Kaleb saw through the real person and only tolerated being around Minus One. It was a blessing to see Kaleb. When we left, Minus One suggested (that means we would do it) we travel to Georgia to visit my mom. It had been five years since I had seen either one of them. I was glad he would do that for me, but in reality, it was for Minus One. I believe he was looking for the future inheritance that might be his when my mom passed away.

Talk about a changed person when he met my mom and her husband. He carried the suitcases in and held the door open for all of us. He engaged in conversation, although the subject was continually turned to something he did or was interested in. I wondered, "Who is this person?" Then I wondered how long this behavior would last. It was not long. After we said our goodbyes the next day, he was back to the usual controlling person. In time, my mom saw through this behavior and removed herself from the trauma and drama of my life. I don't blame her. Who would want to be around an addict and a narcissist?

In the next chapter, I will relate how God protected me and how I realized I would eventually die in this relationship of narcissism and drugs.

*We are what we repeatedly do. Excellence, then,
is not an act, but a habit.
—Will Durant*

Chapter Thirteen

NEAR DEATH

But be sure to fear the Lord and serve him faithfully with all your heart; consider what great things he has done for you.
—*1 Samuel 12:24*

March 2022

Minus One and I had been yelling at each other for several days, maybe weeks. We argued over nothing, it seemed. This time, he was relentless in not letting up with the emotional overload, of which he was an expert. Frankly, I don't know how his grandmother tolerated this behavior. I suspect (believe) she had allowed his actions for most of his life. She was the one who had primarily raised him. He said he was abused by a stepdad, and I get that, but there was no excuse for the behavior he continually displayed.

My dad would call me each day. Fortunately or unfortunately, his phone calls came between bouts. Yet he knew when something was not right. He would hear it in my voice. For six years, I had kept quiet about how difficult and bad my surviving situation was. But he knew. Parents have that sense that tells them when something is not right with their child. What he did not realize was that I was now at the end of my rope. Sometime soon, I would let go. Let go forever. No, I would not knowingly commit suicide because that was not part of my plan. There was a more than better chance I would wake up in heaven if I took enough street drugs.

One thing I have learned over the years is how to sneak to get drugs. I would secretly enter Minus One's grandmother's room and take pain medication and other substances. I frequently got caught. Pain pills, like Percocet and Tylenol with codeine, the pills that are not the breakfast of champions—I took them all. I knew who to call, how to get the drugs delivered, and when. The dealers and I had done this before. We had a delivery system.

The threats and yelling continued to drone on. I could feel I was getting mentally weaker, and I accepted what the result would be. Swallow more numbing street drugs to buffer the hurt.

One time, he poured a liter of soda over my head. Another time, he whipped me with a towel while I was buck naked and sitting on the toilet! And yes, his grandmother was in the house during these incidents. His anger never ceased; it only escalated. His actions had brought my self-worth to the lowest emotional low I had ever experienced. Time to make that drug supplier call. Grandmother's room was now always locked. (That was for my safety, as all medication was kept there.) And yet, he accused me of getting into the room and taking drugs. Not an option anymore. I knew a street supplier who would deliver to the designated spot, and I had some hidden cash. SCORE!

I made the call for some drugs. The street product arrived, but unknown to me, it was lethal. I am sure my supplier could hear the yelling. Minus One and I yelled inside and outside; we were such terrific neighbors. And the neighbors were reluctant to get involved in our issues. Many times, I wondered what the community thought when we were on the front lawn yelling and carrying on like two angry people. It wasn't their battle, and we were not destroying their lives, only ours. I would unknowingly destroy my life soon enough. Just as soon as I could get to the designated hiding place, swallow more than a handful, and numb the hurt.

As always, his actions had provoked me to unleash my emotions without restraint. I had fueled the fire by yelling back, and that had increased the battle. Finally, there was a lull in our fighting, and each of us was hoarse from yelling and screaming.

Time to find my stash. There were more pills than I needed in the batch. (It is always nice when you get extras.) I washed the drugs down with my liquid of choice, a soda this time, but I wished there was something stronger available. More than one swallow's worth, then another.

You never know when someone will mix methamphetamine with a deadly dose of fentanyl. Buying street drugs guarantees you will get trash. As soon as I took the pills, I felt a numbing, floating sensation. This was good and bad. The sensation was unusual because I knew this drug should have taken a little time to work. This meth kicked right in. A mental and physical fog was overtaking me, and my thought was that this drug purchase would not turn out as planned.

Minus One saw this downer attitude and behavior in me and told me I had taken something, which I categorically denied. And another round of fighting started, but I really didn't have it in me to continue the intense battle. I was feeling more than numb, comfortable, floating, and wanted to sleep. My mind continued to become fuzzier and I felt like mush. It was hard for me to see. My eyes would not focus. I knew something was not right, and my mental acuity was slipping away. Because of the way I was feeling, it didn't matter to me anymore. The hurt was being numbed better than it ever had been in the past. I was away on a rainbow cloud. In my altered state, I was just superficially wonderful. Life was beautiful and free from strife. A floating, shadowy world was now my safe and comfortable place. There was not a care in the world for me. The colors were wonderful, so bright and beautiful, things were just perfect. I was smiling for the first time in a long time.

The tunnel I was in was now getting darker and darker. I could hear Minus One yelling at me, but he sounded like he was in a tin can or a cave. It was so easy to shut out everything. My thoughts went into a zombielike peace. All I wanted was to be left alone. That decision was almost fatal.

I was told Minus One took me to an emergency room. It was always our choice of medical treatment. Why go to urgent care and have to pay for part or all of your visit? In the emergency room's waiting room, my breathing stopped, and I was moments away from seeing Jesus. (At this time, I was a Christian believer lite, very lite.) And, no, I didn't see any bright light like some people do with a near-death experience. Seeing me turning blue in the waiting area, Minus One started yelling and creating a scene. He was an expert at doing that to get attention and get his way. For once, this behavior was acceptable.

The medical staff came rushing out, assessed the situation, and concluded I had overdosed on street drugs. Now I was at a life-and-death juncture, which I had no control over. This could have become my fatal and final mistake. I owned it. My decision, no one else's, just me turning blue, not breathing, heart slowing to a stop. But the floating colors that were all around me and had been so beautiful were turning to black. Going, going, almost gone. The medical staff revived me. There was a lot I was never told, or I didn't ask about how I was revived. My dad called it "catch and release." My

Near Death

medical records show I was given four doses of Narcan. The general dosage is one to two. I was close to a heartbeat away from Jesus.

When you hit the bottom, that is precisely when God can work with you the most. *If you let Him.* I had bottomed out, medically, mentally, physically.

Finally, I started breathing. My heart rate, although irregular, became stronger, and I was going to live. Live with the hurt of my life situation. But change would come in the next forty-eight hours. I had already decided I needed to get into the rehabilitation program. The day before all the emergency room ruckus, I had gulped down some drugs. That resulted in me missing my intake appointment. I wanted to get into some program just to get away from Minus One and get some relief. Relief from the consistent badgering, belittling, and berating, not counting the yelling and screaming that was always a part of our lives. I had chosen one in the area that looked good. They would take my insurance. I would now go to that rehab upon my discharge.

Minus One, who worked for the airline, had gotten my father a standby ticket, and Dad flew in to see me. I can only imagine what was going through his mind when he received a late-night call saying I had quit breathing. I imagine I was a physical mess. Being a mess of emotions, I didn't care about anything. Dad and I talked about the emotional mess that he was in after the late-night phone call. Addiction is a boulder in a puddle. You affect people and family more than you realize.

Here is how God works: The airlines granted the standby ticket, which was the last seat on the flight. Dad arrived late at night on the second day. He saw me around midnight after his flight. Visiting hours were over, but the hospital granted him permission to be with me for a few minutes. Not that I recall seeing him. I was still going in and out of consciousness.

Like I have said before, I could let stupid off the leash and I did. (How many times had this happened?)

I remember nothing until leaving the hospital, and that is a foggy, clouded memory. There is no memory of seeing Dad the night he arrived. He was there when I was released. I was wondering why he came to see me, then I realized I was in the intensive care unit! It took me a few minutes to understand the explanation as to why I was there. I was told what I had done and how close to fatal it had been for me. Welcome to the final, fatal step of addiction.

Let me be clear, from all the drugs I have ingested in my life, I should not be alive. Why is God keeping me here on earth? I don't know. This I know: my God is sovereign. He knows my time to come to Him. I have tried to arrange an earlier time, not because I want to but because of addiction. He has protected me, kept me safe. He loves me unconditionally; I am learning to do the same for myself and for Him. He has a plan for the rest of my life, and I am willing and wanting to submit to His authority and will for my life.

Not that submission will be easy for me. I am stubborn. Learning to let go of my pride, being willing to hear His plan, and allowing that process to be implemented is a challenge for me. Perhaps writing this book with my dad is the start of a new path for me. I pray it is. Leaving a life of habitual destruction, leaving a negative life behind, is difficult. However, I know it can be done. There are many success stories about being released from addiction. I imagine there are more stories about fatality from addiction. That is the realm that Satan works in. He is an expert in deception. Chemicals deceived me for over thirty years, making me believe they solved the issue of coping with life. They did not, believe me.

After I was discharged from the hospital, we went back to Minus One's grandmother's house to get my clothes and medications. (You should see that list of meds! I was hooked on legal drugs too.) When you go into a rehabilitation facility, you take just the minimal of essentials. You are there to heal and get redirected to a positive and better life. You don't need a lot of stuff. This is the time your mental and physical stuffing gets taken out and replaced with better stuffing.

Many times, more than I can count, I was a "black bag lady." I packed what I needed to take in a black garbage bag. *Garbage* being the key word. I felt like garbage, my personal items were "garbage," not a positive self-worth image.

I shuffled to the car. As the door to the vehicle closed, I remember thinking, *This time it better work. I don't feel there are many more chances for catch and release.* Minus One's mom was taking me to rehab because Minus One could not know where I was going. (Like that stayed a secret.) Dad was coming along. I would be there for four to five weeks of intensive therapy. For once, I looked forward to getting better, yet I dreaded going, once again, back into rehab. Been there, done that, didn't work.

Would rehab work this time? I wanted to think it would, but from experience, I knew I had a lousy track record of success. Would I be willing to accept the treatment deal with the evil dragons that hounded me? I didn't know, but this time, I felt I was going to try, that I would be willing to work the program for myself. All the other times it had been for others. That change in thought was new to me. I felt that my old ways would creep up, but this time I would slay each dragon one at a time. I would become the storm. I would be the dragon slayer.

The two most important days in your life are the day you're born and the day you find out why.
—*Mark Twain*

Chapter Fourteen

REHABILITATION IN SAN ANTONIO

*The Lord himself goes before you and will be with you;
he will never leave you nor forsake you. Do not be afraid;
do not be discouraged.*
—Deuteronomy 31:8

So I overdosed, almost died, and would have if I had not been in the emergency room when I quit breathing. I remember nothing after swallowing my ill-gotten drugs. According to the ER personnel, I was a mess. There is a video of me being a zombie in a wheelchair. (I slobber really well.) If you have seen any of the news reports of all the drug users living on the streets, that was me. I was completely out of it, a completely addicted druggie waiting to take my final breath.

My dad says God caught and released me as a way of warning, and if it happens again, I may not be released, and I will die.

I don't remember seeing my dad when he flew in from Colorado to Texas. He came to the ICU that night around midnight to see me. From what I am told, I was a barely surviving mess. But I was alive, and my resolve to go to rehab was stronger than ever before.

After the ICU released me, I went directly to rehab. I realize now that this was the first time I wanted to be treated. All the other rehab treatments had been because others, a former husband, mom, or the courts, had directed me there. I had just known I didn't need any of this rehabilitation babble. But I had gone, grudgingly, just to satisfy others. Now, there is an attitude worth getting rid of.

This time, the ride to rehab was as silent as a coffin. My father carried on some form of conversation, but neither my physical nor mental states were really engaged in any conversation that was worth having. I was alive, safe, and "recovering" but in an altered zombie state. There is not much I remember about the ride to rehab. Cars whirred by on the interstate, buildings whizzed past the passenger window. I stared out the car window, not connecting to anything. Reality would arrive later, after I had been at the rehabilitation center for a few days.

We pulled into the rehab center. *It looks OK,* I thought. *Welcome home again for the first time, again.* How many times had I been down the rehab road? Was it three, no, maybe four, five times? You would think something would take hold and correct this self-destructive behavior.

Here is a clue: you have to want to be there. You must take part in the program and absorb, learn what is being presented. Participating by sharing is also a fulcrum of the process. Had I done that in the past? No. I hoped this time would be the last time for rehab and that the program would be different. Time would tell. Once again, I was doing time.

I took a shower at the rehab center and remembered some of what had happened. The reflection in the mirror struck me with how drawn and stressed I looked. There were gray bags under my eyes, and my skin had taken on a pale shade of warmed over. My looks reflected the appearance of a druggie who had almost died. If the mirror could reveal what I was like on the inside, that would be different. Inside I was an emotional black goo. Like a bowl of spaghetti, my feelings were all tangled up together. Once again, I was traveling down the rehab road, not that all rehab centers are the same; believe me, they are not. I felt and hoped that this one was going to be better. As I lay down for a nap, I thought that all I had to do was be a willing part of the program. This was a new, even positive thought.

Rehab was comprised of several modules. The program at this center included group therapy, individual counseling, and writing your life story. Meals were a social time, then there were a few outings away from the center. I was not to have any contact with my "outside world" for several weeks. We were allowed our phones at certain times. However, visitors were not allowed. That was more than fine with me because I didn't want to talk to, see, or interact with Minus One. He was part and parcel of the reason for what happened and why I was here. Anyway, my cell phone was not in my possession when I was in rehab. That kept me from contacting the outside world.

The counselors saw exactly who Minus One was and warned me about any contact with him. (Did I listen? No, not in the beginning.) One counselor got his demeanor immediately. She had lived through the same circumstance that I had. However, Minus One didn't pay any attention to the rules. He would call, come by, and drop off packages (love bombs, again) for me. Always continuing to set the emotional hooks that I was trying to release.

He would show up at the center with stuffed animals, flowers, candy, cards, and his usual nauseating self: quite the nuisance. He tried to bring things he knew would keep me hooked. He was not to be detoured; narcissists are like that. They are hound dogs. Once they get your scent, they are on your trail.

Once, when we were on an outing away from the center, he found out where we were and showed up. I had been feeling a sense of peace. I was relaxed watching the ducks swim, the sun warming me where I was sitting. I was momentarily at peace. I felt safe. Then I heard him calling my name, and then his overbearing presence shattered that comfortable outing. My stomach leaped into my throat, bile rose, and fear and unbelief were instantly present. I didn't know what would happen. All I could feel was a complete sense of invasion. It was my fault. I had phone privileges, and he had gotten the location of where we were going and at what time from me. He brought "our" two dogs, and his behavior also brought me discipline from the counselors on duty. The counselors directed him to leave. He did, but the damage was done. I had a temporary setback. Plus this incident was not fair to the other residents, as I am sure they experienced emotional trauma. (Many addicts choose the same type of personality in their friendships and relationships.)

The counselor talked to me. I admitted I was incorrect in saying where we were going, but a narcissist can get information out of you. They are experts in pulling out information to use against you. The dog trick was nice, however hurtful. In thinking back, I believe Minus One was not there to support me but to shatter the progress I was making.

During the group gathering that night, people challenged me with questions and comments: How can you still be with someone like that? What were you thinking? You are better than that and deserve someone who loves you. He should have known better.

However, Minus One believed the rules never applied to him. OK, I have had that same thinking too, but therapy is now showing me differently. That incident was a revelation for me.

There were more lessons I learned that day. My group showed compassion, support, love for me, but most of all, understanding and forgiveness. I realized they cared for me, for who I was. Now I needed to care for myself, and that was happening, ever so slowly. The rehab staff reexplained the rules, and I would be on my guard when talking to Minus One. Actually, I thought I should never talk to him, but I was still weak and needy. When you are climbing out of the emotional pit of any addiction, the walls are slippery and there are few handholds for you to grab. You need to be willing to reach up and grab the healing hand of Jesus. At some point, you finally wake up to that realization.

There was a set routine in rehab and counseling. Our days started at seven o'clock, and we were to be in bed at ten in the evening. There were the sessions we attended, meals, outings, fellowship time, and AA, which would come to the building. Each piece of the process was another brick in our healing. My dad has continued to tell me over the many years that if you use the same bricks, you will build the same structure. I was an expert at this, but now I wanted to build a new me with a new set of bricks.

For once, I was in a program that made sense to me. I believe the other programs had merit, but I was reluctant to embrace change. This time was different. There is a wonderful song titled "Something Beautiful" written by Bill and Gloria Gaither that relates to how Christ sees you. Every day, I continue to strive to reach this new standard in my life, and I know this will be a lifetime process. I will continue to strive to be more like Christ in me. Please allow me to share the lyrics with you from "Something Beautiful."

Something beautiful, something good
All my confusion He understood.
All I had to offer Him was brokenness and strife
But he made something beautiful in my life
If there ever were dreams
That were lofty and noble
They were my dreams at the start
And hope for life's best were the hopes
That I harbor down deep in my heart
But my dreams turned to ashes
And my castles all crumbled, my fortune turned to loss
So I wrapped it all in the rags of life
And laid it at the cross.[5]

A journey through rehab is not a straight course or a stroll through a park. You must work the process, and the process can and many times will be excruciating. There is the peeling back of your life. Like a scientist or a surgeon, you are personally and publicly taking apart your life, brick by brick, and looking at your circumstances. Examining who you are, discovering what you want to become, and finding a path and plan to follow. There are no simple emotional road maps or comfortable GPS routes to follow. You must, through certified counseling and group support, create your healing and hike to the top of your mountain. I believe, when an addict finds recovery, they know and marvel at the view of their future.

Sometimes you get an offhand compliment that makes your day. After the Minus One park incident, I was chiding myself (I can be good at that) about not being careful about giving out information that could hurt me as well as the group at rehab. We were sitting around our usual circle. This was a mixed group, which gave a different perspective. I was internalizing and coasting on the outside edge of the session, when I heard this person address me. What he said changed my outlook to a more positive outlook. "Jen, I am not coming on to you, but I need to say this. When you are in the room, you light up the room, and your smile brightens the room even more."

I could not comprehend what he was saying. Was this a compliment? I didn't get those and rarely received any positive remarks. Even when I was married, nothing but flat remarks, and Minus One, well, you know about that; he was the expert on negativity.

Being in a rehab situation was like being in a gumball machine. We were all there for the same reason, but each of us had a different addictive color for our own physiological condition. However, the common thread was addiction, hopefully leading to a goal of healing. There was an opportunity to find a new, productive life path, if we chose. All of us were there because of what we did in the past, and the sad part is, many of us would fall back into the same destructive behavior again. Addiction is like that: get clean, go dirty, get clean, go dirty again and again. Many times, the dirty will cause earthly dirt to be placed over you forever. All of us there knew of someone who hadn't made it. We could see our future in their past, but it did not stop us from going back time and time again.

I have decided I will be free of addiction. My future will be as a recovering addict and alcoholic. Being a drug-dependent person is and will be part of my past. Yes, I have said this before, many times. I didn't believe or mean it then; I do now. When you are scared to death, you handle life differently. Calling on Jesus to get on board and to keep my eyes on Him, that is my life goal. When Peter stepped out of the boat onto the water, he kept his eyes on Jesus. Looking away resulted in him taking a swimming lesson and Jesus reaching out and rescuing him (Matthew 14:25–31). I have taken my eyes off Jesus more times than I can count. I am working to change that in my life. This I know: He has never taken His eyes off me.

After five weeks, it was time for me to be released from rehab. My counselor and my dad talked a lot, from what I learned. She told him clearly that if I stayed in San Antonio, I would not live. So dad and my bonus mom, once again, came, took me in, and furnished me with a peaceful and safe place to live. Meals on the table, support, and counseling. That didn't last long. I let stupid out of the yard once again.

Make sure your worst enemy doesn't live between your own two ears.
—Laird Hamilton

Chapter Fifteen

Going Home

Going Back

~~~

Love does not delight in evil but rejoices with the truth. It always protects, always trusts, always hopes, always perseveres.
—*1 Corinthians 13:6–7*

Dad Speaking

I picked Jen up from the rehab center on a sunny and warm Friday. It was a delight to see my daughter, to hug her and know she was coming home. The warmth of the day and the comfort of a family reunion brought a good and completed feeling. I believed Jen's life was being turned around.

Our conversation was positive. I could sense that there was a new outlook, direction, and commitment with Jen. She was focused and was leaving the past behind. We drove to a chaplain friend's house about five hours away. Minus One kept calling Jen as we traveled, every day hounding her, wanting to know what was happening. Each call became an irritant to me. She was away from him, done and gone. Or so all of us thought. Time would tell us differently.

Our first night was one of relief and comfort. This chaplain couple we stayed with overnight knew how to help release the stress and pressure from any situation. The dinner was something Jen could eat. (Her dentures prevent her from eating a lot of foods that are difficult to chew.) According to this couple, this chicken dish was a staple for potlucks at church. I think, with Jen taking seconds and almost thirds, it was definitely a hit. The conversation over dinner was pleasant and comfortable. Jen could share her experiences over the past six years. They already knew most of the story, but having her tell it directly, I feel, helped Jen release more of the past.

I didn't want to leave the next day, as the time invested there was precious to both of us. However, schedules needed to be met and addressed, and my son was expecting us by nightfall. The drive would take most of the day; however, I planned a daughter-daddy event that turned into a couple of events because of a father's lead accelerator foot!

As we traveled, Jen and I talked at length about her time in rehab and the situation with Minus One. Instead of sleeping all the time, she was open about her life experiences. That was when I heard God telling me a book should be written so that others would know the dangers of addiction.

We stopped at a shopping center that sported an outdoor store and a shoe store. Because Jen has feet problems, the shoe store was somewhere she needed to go to get shoes that would help her walk. MS does that: it wreaks havoc on a person's body.

We took in an aviation museum. Just a time to walk around together, talk, share, reset. Over the past several decades, we hadn't had time for the two of us. Museums are a perfect place to wander, talk, and learn to appreciate the past.

Staying at our youngest son's house would also be a healing and safe time for Jen. Watching and listening to all the family talk and the understanding, love, and support that was being doled out made such a difference for Jen. She was not used to unconditional love.

We finally arrived at our home in time for dinner: enchiladas—Jennifer's favorite dish that Barb could make for her. Again, food was devoured and love was poured out as the evening progressed.

In the rose-colored glasses of my mind, things were going great. Jen had a job just down the street. She was in virtual therapy and getting healed. However, Minus One continued to hound her with calls many times a day. Some I knew about, many I didn't, as he would call her at work. Then the proposal of coming back to San Antonio "for a few days" was offered. Jen accepted. The one trip turned into a few more, with each trip extending another day or so. Minus One was working his narcissistic manipulation, reeling her back ever so slowly into his nefarious grip.

We were at the airport saying goodbye, and I said I would see her in a few days, which I believe she felt would be the case. It wasn't. Once more, Jen fell into the trap, enticed by the emotional hooks. On the appointed day of her return, she said she was staying "a few more days." Barb knew she was not coming back. She tried to let me know easily, but I didn't comprehend what she was saying.

Then a text came from Jen stating she was going to stay with Minus One. That text severed my loving heart for my daughter. Couldn't she have called so we could talk about this? I felt betrayed, lied to, manipulated, and I believed this was also the case for Jen. Minus One had won this round. Jen was an adult, it was her choice, well, his choice. Later, I learned she had been pressured into that decision.

This is a text I received from Jen a few days later.

> I am going into this with my eyes wide open. I believe we can make a go of this being sober (both of us). And if it doesn't work and backfires on me, I will at least know that I tried and won't wonder what could have been.
>
> He is being the person I met when we first got together. No lies, no deception and hiding what's really going on my side. He promises me that no name calling and yelling. Honesty, love, and respect. If I don't try, I will never know.

Then, a day later, this text arrived. I asked her if she had really thought this decision through, and she said she had. I was not convinced in any way. All that could be done now was pray.

> Yes. We have. I know we both need to work on our / my/ his issues. I opened up to him about a lot of things I've been hiding and burying. He also did the same. We are on even ground. I feel in my heart that he deserves a sober Jen. I want to give it another chance. I want to stay. I know this hurts you. And Barbie and the family. For this I'm sorry. I've been praying about it. Talked to my therapist and counselor, also my support group. I still honor the commitment I've made with you and the book. I can come there anytime I'm off. This is really hard for me, but I'm doing this whole honestly and upfront. No matter how hard it is, I have to be truthful. It's really hard. I love you a lot and don't want to hurt you.

Hurt? Yes. Forgiveness and concern for Jen? Absolutely. Fear for my daughter's safety? Every second of each day. My nightly prayer was that God would protect her and keep her safe. God answers prayers, sometimes the way we would like and other times not. In Jen's case, He kept His hand of protection on her; she was as safe as she could be. However, that would change in the coming year.

I found out Jen had called her supervisor at the convenience store where she had a job and had told her of this decision the day before I found out. Looking back, there was so much cohesion, so much manipulation from Minus One. He said she could have a job as a caregiver for a disabled person. But the hourly wage was split between Jennifer and Minus One. Each day soured more and more. He constructed the prison; Minus One put Jen in it, for now, and discarded the key.

As I have previously mentioned, my prayer was for Jen's protection and safety. My prayers are still continuing, and this passage from Psalms becomes more written upon my heart every day. Psalm 91:10–11: "No harm will overtake you, no disaster will come near your tent. For he will command his angels concerning you to guard you in all your ways."

There are many other verses that offer and show God's protection in our dangerous circumstances of life. I also offer you this verse if you are praying for yourself or someone who is in danger. Psalm 32:8: "I will instruct you and teach you in the way you should go; I will counsel you with my loving eye on you."

Yet it is our responsibility to listen for and implement God's will. Knowing her decision was going to result in her being back in the same miry pit she was previously in stabbed my father's heart. But Jen was an adult, she had free will, and I believe that God and I wept together over her decision. There was nothing I could do, only pray, wait, and hope she would come to see the mistake she had made.

Being back with Minus One gave him a heightened sense of control over Jen. She was under his spell and discipline. Once again, Jen joined him in indulging in various activities like smoking weed, traveling to casinos, and getting high on drugs. That was the lifestyle. Nothing like when she was with family. Now she had no family except Minus One and his grandmother. She found herself trapped, attempting to prove the relationship would work.

He made promises that she could continue her virtual counseling, but that didn't happen. He promised they would find a church and attend. This never happened. He promised he would be kind, loving, gracious, and understanding—not a chance. A narcissist creates support for their victim. That is the foundation of a narcissistic relationship. The support is for the narcissist, not the "partner." There is not a partnership, only one person matters: the other person is there for the convenience of the narcissist.

Their relationship continued to spiral down like a funnel from a tornado. I would call, and the storm would continue to brew. From what I know, the fighting became more and more intense, as Minus One wanted more "support" from Jen. A light in a dark tunnel was still there, as Jen would recall being in a positive and safe environment. I believe she would compare the two living lifestyles and wonder about her decision.

Twice, that I know of, they flew to Colorado; you know why, dope. And there was never time for Jen and I (with Minus One lurking in the background) to visit, even for an hour. If we were to meet, he hung around like low-hanging rotten fruit on a tree. I believe that was the beginning of Jen's realization that he was taking her away from her family, imprisoning her as his family. She had no interaction with other people.

One trip they traveled to Colorado by car. They flew back to Texas and flew back to Colorado, then drove home. Why, you ask, would that be a plan? Simple answer: it is easier to transport weed in a car than to carry it on a commercial flight. Here was the concern: a Texas licensed car traveling through known cities that sold this product and across state lines. Remember Jen's record: if she got stopped and caught, that would place her—once again—back in jail. As a third offense, Jen would be back in federal prison. Minus One didn't see or care about the situation.

Jen and I talked about this possibility, but to no avail. It was about this time that the situation further soured. Minus One started to strike out and hit Jen. "It was my fault," she told me. "I angered him, and he responded by striking me. He punched me hard in the arm."

It was decision time for Jen, stay or go. To stay would offer the opportunity for increased violence, which happened. To leave would require her taking charge, planning, and implementing a plan. Minus One always hung around when we talked on the phone. He would be within hearing range, so using texts and deleting the texts was the only option.

We discussed and agreed upon a date and then laid out plans. Barb and I talked at length about how our life would be affected. We knew, once again, we would have demands on our time, a changing of schedules to support Jen's needs, appointments, and errands. Our one-on-one time would now add another person's schedule. We would arrange another schedule in an already complicated daily routine. However, to love unconditionally, to bring your children or anyone you are involved with to a better place, is a part of God's plan. Isn't that the reason Jesus came from His Father to earth, to create a salvation bridge? To save people for eternity, and that absolutely must include family. If Jesus's first miracle was at a wedding, there was something to be learned from this event. Family is paramount for a solid, secure foundation in anyone's life. Decision made, extraction planned.

Texts were going back and forth as Jen and I read them and Jen deleted them while putting final plans into place. Every correspondence was directed to take her away from physical and emotional trauma that was her life. What I saw in our conversations was a new determination in Jen's demeanor. She wanted out; she longed to be healed. It was finally time. Time for Jen to become Jen. Buried deep in her soul was a woman-child longing for freedom and safety. Longing to submit to the will of God.

But first, she needed to depart from Minus One. A final rodeo needed to happen, and then healing, precious healing, would begin. That extraction, rescue (what number was this deliverance, three or four?), would happen two weeks in the future. Time, for me, never moved more slowly, fourteen days, 336 hours. The clock moved forward, but not at the speed a father would have liked. Yet all was in God's timing, and His schedule is not ours. Jesus clearly states this when He says, "Therefore keep watch because you do not know when the owner of the house will come back—whether in the evening, or at midnight, or when the rooster crows, or at dawn" (Mark 13:35). So I impatiently waited for the appointed time.

Finally, the day arrived. The next chapter is Jen's version of her extraction.

> *Doubt is a killer. You just have to know who you are and what you stand for.*
> *—Jennifer Lopez*

Chapter Sixteen

GETTING OUT

HOMEWARD BOUND

―∽―

He has called me by name and I am His!
—Isaiah 43:1 (author's paraphrase)

I am more than a conqueror in all things,
for nothing can separate me from God's love!
—Romans 8:37, 39 (author's paraphrase)

Hi, this is Jennifer, with more of the story about coming home.

Sometimes it takes one more violent incident to make or allow a person to decide enough is enough. Perhaps, in the past, small things have happened that made you think, but you ignored them. Or believed it wouldn't happen again. Not true; once violence starts, violence will continue, and it will escalate. To definitely decide to leave is the best way to stop this behavior.

Minus One (I like what my dad named him) slugged me in the arm (left a bruise, but he said he was just "playing around"). A few days later, he slapped me hard on the back of my head. I knew it was time to leave.

Getting Out

Now, leaving sounds simple. It is not. Plans have to be made but not written, lest the person you are leaving finds them, and you know what will happen then. I clandestinely communicated every aspect of the plan with my dad. We set a time and a date, not as soon as I wanted it to happen, but I had to be released from medical treatment, and I also had one more infusion for my MS that I needed to take.

It is difficult to leave a six-year relationship. However, it is crucial to leave a noxious relationship, especially when that person has convinced you that you are the crazy one. Deep down, inside my soul, I knew I was not insane even though I was told every day that there was something, or everything, wrong with me. After a while, I believed what I was told. However, God continued to protect me day after day, year after year. I am aware of that now. I can look back and see the emotional destruction that this "partner" caused me.

I can see when all my friends quit calling me or didn't respond to me when I reached out. Narcissists isolate you by cutting off communication with people from your past and your family. I temporally lost my friends—those who supported me, all gone. But not now. I am slowly rebuilding positive former relationships and looking for new Christian friends. Emphasis on the word *Christian*. I now have boundaries and standards that I didn't possess before.

Back to my escape. Yes, *escape* is the right word. You just don't walk away, you run. Run as fast as you can. I shared my situation and the plans that we were making to escape with my MS physician during my office visit. She said, "I have only one word for you, 'Run.' "

Dad and I continued to set a plan for departure. We could not openly talk, so texting became the best communication tool to use. I would receive a text from him, commit it to memory, and immediately delete it. We did this for over two weeks. Each day became more and more risky as we completed what needed to be accomplished for my escape. I found out leaving a narcissist involves more than just walking away. They will continue to "love bomb, gift bomb" you. Breaking off all communication is primary. You have heard the phrase give them an inch and they will take a mile. Narcissists put you down and discourage you, even when you're being supportive. You give that emotional inch and they take your life. That is what I finally realized, almost too late.

Dad and I had talked back and forth for the six years I was with Minus One. He knew this was a failed relationship from the beginning. He would always encourage me to leave. "Get to a halfway house, get on a plane, a bus, just get out." Why did I stay? Because I believed I could fix him. I am a person who will give and give until there is nothing to give, and then I will figure a way to give anyway. Narcissists look (*hunt* would be a better word) for this type of subservient, giving, solving personality. A narcissistic person does not know how to love. They find a person who will love them and commit to them. It is a hunt for their own validation. The lower the self-worth of a potential "partner," the easier the manipulation.

Time moved slower and slower in the two weeks of planning. Finally, the date of leaving was here.

On a Thursday, Dad left Colorado for Texas. He was planning on staying at my bonus brother's home in north Texas. The next day, both of them would drive to south Texas, stay the night, and extract, *rescue*, me, then we would drive back to my bonus brother's home for the evening. The following night, I would be in Colorado. Finally safe, and that is what I wanted to believe.

We developed a coded text message that would let me know they were in the motel and then, the next morning, another neutral message that they were in place to come and get me.

I needed to have what I could take ready to go. There was a problem. Where should I put or hide my clothes to avoid them being discovered? It was two weeks of sneaking and setting the process in motion. I devised a plan, organized my belongings in black garbage bags, and hoped their discovery would be avoided. The bags were placed outside of the house in the last few days in an area where I knew Minus One would not look. If he discovered them, I would have to deal with the situation. I was sorting and selecting what I wanted to take. He asked me what I was doing, which was continual with everything I did. I replied that it was time to store my seasonal clothes and I that was giving away what I didn't wear or need. I've done a garbage bag move before—this wasn't the first time—but I believed this was the last time.

The last phase of the escape plan was simple. I would wait until he went into his home office to work at 8:30 in the morning. At 9:15, my brother and dad would show up, and I would slip out the back door, gather my garbage bags, and get them in the car. And we would be gone. Simple plans can change, and this one did. However, God was in control and allowed me to take charge of what I needed to do. God gives you the strength you need at the time required. Like David and Goliath, I was ready to sling the final stone.

I got my morning text, an hour ahead of time!

"I am not ready" was my response. I thought I was ready, but reality kicked in, and the escape plan was being implemented.

Dad had asked for the police to be present when I left. After a meeting between my dad, my brother, and the authorities, a squad car showed up at the house I was escaping from. None of us expected them to show up as quickly as they did.

Dad called and told me it was "go time." We were on the police department's schedule. The police knocked on the door as I hung up from talking to my dad!

Minus One was not at work. Now we were dancing around a potential, maybe violent, conflict. And then there was the issue of him smoking an illegal product. He was smoking what they call a blunt (a marijuana cigar). The presence of the police caused him to freak out and run to hide the marijuana. (Question: how do you hide the smell of marijuana?)

It is interesting that when you look to our Lord and Savior, your eyes are opened to the circumstance you are in. Like Saul in the Bible, my scales were removed. I was seeing clearly, and I did not like what I saw or what I smelled.

"Why are the police at our door?" Minus One asked. I looked him directly in the eye, mustering all the authority and courage I could, took a breath, and said, "Because I am leaving." This was the beginning of my freedom from all the emotional and physical trauma I had subjected myself to.

"OK, when?" he asked.

"Right now," I replied as I opened the door.

Then the two-year-old child came out in him as he flopped on the floor, hugging my legs, pleading with me not to go. *Too late,* I thought. Because I was not giving in or giving him sympathy, he went yelling and crying to his grandmother. His grandmother always slept late, but that didn't matter. He got her up and continued to cry and play the poor-little-boy victim card.

"Can't you wait until my heart surgery is over? I am going to die in surgery anyway," the crying man-child wailed. "Then you will have my life insurance money." The scene became a full-blown trauma drama, with both Minus One and his grandmother saying I was being manipulated by my father and his family. I thought, *The manipulation was not from*

Getting Out

family but from the controlling boy-not-turned-man I have been with for six trauma-filled years.

I looked out the storm door again. Now there were two police cars and three officers. Things had the potential to escalate out of control. But with three officers, a mad dad, and a protective brother, Minus One did the math. Five to one is not the best of odds to try anything. Later, I found out Dad had told the first responding officer about the hotheaded assault record and conviction of Minus One. That was the reason another squad car with two officers showed up. Minus One kept pleading with me to "just stay a few more days."

The police officers were watching the situation to see if Minus One was going to escalate the situation. They were getting irritated about me being in the house and not being allowed to leave.

He kept begging and pleading with me, making more and more promises that he would break. I told the boy-child, "Either you back off and let me go now, or the police are coming in here, and that will not be good for you. You don't want that." Because the house always smelled of pot, that statement carried weight.

During this time Dad and my brother were taking all the black bags and the one suitcase and backpack that were hidden outside and getting them in the car. One more sweep through the house and a goodbye to the dogs. (They had known something was happening the night before, as they had cuddled more than usual.)

I was out the door, into the car, and here comes Minus One still pleading, crying, and carrying on. To be able to leave, I had to tell him we were going to breakfast. Well, we went to breakfast. I imagine he finally realized we were not coming back. We were miles down the road, and all of my six years of trauma were in the rearview mirror. Now a new secure life was in my future.

Have you ever torn off a bandage from a wound? When you rip an emotional bandage from yourself, you feel deep pain and trauma. The bandage was off, but the scar would be there for a long time. Each mile we traveled compounded the guilt he had programmed me to feel. The mental ghosts of doubt started in on me. *Maybe I should have given him one more chance. He had some positive qualities. He looked so sad and was crying.* The thoughts went on and on. They haunted me. Someone had manipulated me into unreasonable submission.

Leaving was traumatic but necessary. Staying would have prevented me from becoming the person God wants me to be. And I am thankful for my heavenly Father keeping me safe and protected over the years I was deep in the miry pit of the narcissistic relationship. I am thankful for my dad and my brother being willing, once again, to commit to rescuing me. Rescuing, yes. This situation required an extraction and a rescue. I now can, through therapy, counseling, and family support, address the issues that caused me to make choices that were not in my best interests, choices that allowed others to take advantage of me. The road ahead will be fraught with challenges as I peel back the layers of emotional lies that I embraced.

Am I scared about what I will find out? You bet I am, but I am ready to "put on the full armor of God" (Ephesians 6:11) so that I can make my stand against the devil's schemes that have ruled my life for the past four decades. I know the introspective journey will be challenging. However, to slay the dragons that have controlled your life, you must confront every one. Slay each monster, bury it, move on to the next dragon, and repeat the process. With each victory comes another level of peace and control of your life.

Getting Out

My goal is to serve God with all of my heart for the amount of time I have on earth. I pray this journey that I am on will help you understand the dangers of the devil in your life. To avoid a life of despair, sin, drugs, and deception.

As my dad always says, "Continue to continue, to trust Jesus." I am, and I am eager to see where He leads. Finally, after about four decades of addiction, abuse, self-denial, and refusing to follow God's will, I can see a positive direction in my life. I am moving on, not looking back. "But Lot's wife looked back [yearning for what was in the past], and she became a pillar of salt" (Genesis 19:26).

Some people want it to happen, some wish it would happen, others make it happen.
—Michael Jordan

Chapter Seventeen

THE FUTURE

*Even to your old age and gray hairs
I am he, I am he who will sustain you.
I have made you and I will carry you;
I will sustain you and I will rescue you.
—Isaiah 46:4*

We don't know our future. That is for God to know. Disregarding God's will allows Satan to enter and control our lives. So many people fall into this deceitful web of lies and negative direction. Then they wonder why there is no joy in their lives. The challenges overwhelm them. They continue to fall into a quicksand of existence, not knowing the depth of despair they are continually living in. That was me, and by the grace of God, I am not living that life anymore.

Yes, I will face temptation because once you become an addict, you will always be an addict. Alcoholics Anonymous (AA) has a statement that you are always a recovering alcoholic. I believe that is true for a drug addict as well. AA has meetings in almost every city in the USA. Narcotics Anonymous (NA) is another organization that addresses individuals with past addictions. My mom has been going to NA meetings for many years, and I believe that has helped her to deal with and sometimes understand what I have gone through. People can't grasp the extent of the damage they've done to themselves

The Future

until they're completely free from drugs or alcohol. Of course, I will never fully realize the extent of sorrow, hurt, and helplessness I have burdened my loved ones with.

I do not know the tears of sorrow I caused for my dad. The anger that my mom has and had toward me. The hurt from my marriage that resulted in divorce due to my life choices. Or the child from whom I am estranged. Actions have consequences, and I own the actions of my life. However, our God is a God of unconditional love and more than one chance. Colossians 1:13 states, "For he has rescued us from the dominion of darkness and brought us into the kingdom of the Son he loves." I cannot count the Colossians moments in my life. There are way too many to count. And now it does not matter. Many years ago, I professed my faith in Jesus Christ.

I became a child of God when my father came to Florida, and he baptized me. I was continuing to spiral down more and more, but I was desperate for a better life. Not fully trusting Jesus allowed the evil one to dominate my addicted life. As you have read, my life was not a fairy tale, nor was I a princess. A court jester might be a better description of what I was. *Was* is the key word. I am changing, being transformed from a caterpillar into a beautiful butterfly.

This transformation has taken a lifetime. But our Lord is a patient and loving Lord. He suffers when we suffer, rejoices when we rejoice. However, we have this thing called free will. There are so many times I wish God would have just butt kicked me down the right path. But the complete part of His love for us is allowing us to make choices. Many times, the decisions we make are not for our own good or safety.

I have said before and will state many, many times again, choices create consequences. You do stupid things, stupid things happen to you. Drink and drive, get in a wreck, receive a ticket for drunk driving. Do drugs, get hooked, become an addict. Steal something small, start stealing larger things, get caught, go to jail. Get into a fight, get bruises, maybe lose a tooth.

All the above seems black and white because it is. God gave us the Ten Commandments, black and white. They are NOT ten suggestions. Here is the list because I will not assume you have read or memorized them. If you have done both, congratulations, read them again. If you have not read what God is saying, do not, I repeat, DO NOT skip this part. I did and now you know my life story.

1. You shall have no other gods before me.
2. You shall not make idols and worship them.
3. You shall not take the name of the Lord your God in vain.
4. Remember the Sabbath day, to keep it holy.
5. Honor your father and your mother.
6. You shall not commit murder.
7. You shall not commit adultery.
8. You shall not steal.
9. You shall not bear false witness against your neighbor.
10. You shall not covet (Exodus 20:3–17, author's paraphrase).

Now that you have read them, read them again.

OK, finalizing my life, let me take you through a laundry list of my former life and how I used to live in opposition to the Ten Commandments.

Number One - No Gods before Me: Alcohol and drugs were my gods. I worshiped them, craved their soothing pleasure.

Number Two - Idols: Music, rockstars—some I idolized.

Number Three - Taking the Lord's Name in Vain: I used the Lord's name so many times. Then there was the swearing. I could keep up with the best of them. Anger plays into cursing. I was mad, and my mouth definitely defined my anger.

Number Four - Keep the Sabbath Day: I didn't go to church, and I didn't worship God—I didn't need that Christian "stuff." Yes, I knew Jesus, but Satan had a hold on me. I had to work to get my fixes.

Number Five - Honor Your Parents: There was something I didn't do, and I know it hurt them. I was me, and that was all I needed. Yes, I loved them, but did I know what the commitment of love really meant?

Number Six - Murder: Abortion is murder, plain and simple. I am guilty times two.

Number Seven - Committing Adultery: Guilty as charged. It is important to reserve sex for marriage, not any night of the week with any person. Yes, I could snag a guy anytime I wanted, and that was so wrong. I know that now.

Number Eight - Stealing: Yup, done that. I believed they, or the company, would not miss it, and anyway I needed whatever "it" was.

Number Nine - Lying: When I needed to get out of a sticky situation, I lied. I would not tell the whole truth. I would deny an action. However, when pressed and pushed, I would tell the truth. My bonus mom would get the truth from me. It felt worse in the moment but better later.

Number Ten - Coveting: There is something that is difficult not to do when you see the world spinning around you and people have things you want. Sometimes it was their boyfriend. Sometimes it was wishing I had a smart phone or watch like they had. Even seeing people dining on a scrumptiously wonderful meal and wanting it for myself. Yes, I have coveted.

We have all fallen short of the love, grace, and mercy of God. Yet there is hope, eternal hope. Most addicts cannot see any hope for their future, just another drink, fix, or hookup. That, dear reader, is Satan worming his way into those lives, setting hooks, and making a date with an eternal destiny that does not have to be.

There is another way: accept Jesus. Accept Him as your Savior. Ask Him into your heart. Are you willing to bet your eternity on something you cannot see but believe in? Sounds crazy, doesn't it? Jesus is waiting for you to trust Him. He is crazy in love with you and wants you to go to be with Him in eternity, timeless in heaven.

The Holy Bible has sixty-six books in it. Contained in those pages is what you need for life (B.I.B.L.E. Basic Instructions Before Leaving Earth). We will all die and face Jesus. It states that plainly in the Bible. Like realtors tell you, it is all about location, location, location. Each of us can make that eternal decision. I have made mine. I know, without a doubt, I am going to heaven. My eternal destination is but a heartbeat away, just like yours.

Once you have taken your final breath on earth and inhaled your first eternal breath, if you have not accepted Jesus, that door is closed. Like all the people who mocked Noah, when the door of the ark was sealed by God, it was over. The floods came, forty days and nights. None of them could tread water that long; could you? I doubt it.

There is a path you can take, a path to your joy, your happiness. Not that Christians don't face trials, temptations, and tribulations—we do—but we have a God who loves, cares, and protects us and gives us strength to persevere, to push forward. Come with me on what has been called the Romans Road. Romans is a book in the Bible that gives you the reason to seek eternity.

The Future

Here we go. Read with all your heart. Your future is being determined by you.

We have all sinned.

Romans 3:10–12, 23: "As it is written: 'There is no one righteous, not even one; there is no one who understands; there is no one who seeks God. All have turned away; they have together become worthless; there is no one who does good, not even one. . . . For all have sinned and fall short of the glory of God."

The price (or consequence) of sin is death.

Romans 6:23: "For the wages of sin is death, but the free gift of God is eternal life in Christ Jesus our Lord."

Jesus Christ died for our sins. He paid the price for our sins.

Romans 5:8: "But God demonstrates his own love for us in this: While we were still sinners, Christ died for us."

We receive salvation and eternal life through faith in Jesus Christ.

Romans 10:9–10, 13: "If you declare with your mouth, 'Jesus is Lord,' and believe in your heart that God raised him from the dead, you will be saved. For it is with your heart that you believe and are justified, and it is with your mouth that you profess your faith and are saved. . . . For 'Everyone who calls on the name of the Lord will be saved.' "

Salvation through Jesus brings us into a relationship of peace with God.

Romans 5:1: "Therefore, since we have been justified through faith, we have peace with God through our Lord Jesus Christ."

Romans 8:1: "Therefore, there is now no condemnation for those who are in Christ Jesus."

Romans 8:38–39: "For I am convinced that neither death nor life, neither angels nor demons, neither the present nor the future, nor any powers, neither height nor depth, nor anything else in all creation, will be able to separate us from the love of God that is in Christ Jesus our Lord."

Yes, life is full of challenges, complications, trials, and suffering, to name a few. You and I know there are other challenges, temptations, and times we will be hurt by someone we love. Every day we have to decide, good and sometimes bad. However, can you even imagine deciding without Jesus's guidance? If you do not believe in Him, of course you can. Could you tell me why you would continue your self-destructive lifestyle? If you have chosen Christ as your Savior. If not, choose Him now. Is this the life choice you want for yourself? Another fix, another drink, another . . . another?

Christians, if you know someone who is in addiction, go to them. Pray for them. You may be their only chance to recover. Get involved. Here is a reality check: I know that if it wasn't for people willing to get in my mess and confront me, I could not have told you the things in my life that I did. I absolutely know there were many people I don't know who were involved in praying for me. My dad, my bonus mom, my mom, and others from churches prayed to our Lord on my behalf because I could not. Or would not.

None of us know what our future brings. I know this. I believe in Jesus as my Lord and Savior. There is a Holy Spirit that dwells in me. (You can read about that in the Bible.) I am

The Future

His child, and I am going to heaven to live a timeless eternity with MY Jesus and Lord. And that is enough for me. What about you?

> *Sow righteousness for yourselves,*
> *reap the fruit of unfailing love,*
> *and break up your unplowed ground;*
> *for it is time to seek the Lord,*
> *until he comes*
> *and showers his righteousness on you.*
> *—Hosea 10:12*

Chapter Eighteen

Getting Help

*Those who know your name trust in you,
for you, Lord, have never forsaken those who seek you.*
—Psalm 9:10

There are many resources available to help someone who is an addict in crisis. My dad says that two presidents, George Washington and Abraham Lincoln, said you cannot believe all that you read on the Internet. I believe he has a point. Bear with me on this. I am in counseling, not just "counseling" but with a certified biblical Christian counselor, which, I believe, is the best choice for healing. Although there are many professional secular counselors who can be of help to you, I would recommend checking online reviews and seeing where they received their education. How long they have been in practice. You might know a person who was under their care: ask them what they thought. These are a few ways to make sure you have chosen the person who will and can help you the most.

There are many books and articles that you can research, and ever-growing lists of websites with information and knowledge. We talked about creating a list for this book. However, information and website links change as the sun rises and sets. So we will not give you a list that will become outdated. There are search engines you can use to find resources. Remember

Getting Help

what my dad said: "You cannot believe all that you read on the Internet." Do your research, ask questions. If the solution seems too good to be true, it probably is. Like drugs, there are more scams out there that can take you in, grind you up, and toss you under the bus.

The one and only solution is to seek Jesus. He has the deepest love for you, more than you deserve. His love is a gift. Trust Jesus. Many addicts have discovered His grace, mercy, and healing power. The success stories would fill volumes of books. Without His protection, this book would have a far more tragic ending instead of a victory and a life saved, now serving His kingdom.

Jesus gave us direction when He said, "But seek first his kingdom and his righteousness, and all these things will be given to you as well" (Matthew 6:33). If we do not seek His direction and His will in our lives, we will crash upon the rocky shores of life. Would it not be better to sail into the loving, safe harbor our Lord has for us? I am not saying getting help, getting clean, and staying clean will be easy. It is not: every day, every moment of the day, there will be temptations. However, when you accept Jesus as your Savior, you are on a winning team for eternity. Avarice, negativity, the helplessness you feel—like morning fog, it all goes away. Your internal Son shines because of the Holy Spirit that now dwells within you. "If you then, though you are evil, know how to give good gifts to your children, how much more will your Father in heaven give the Holy Spirit to those who ask him!" (Luke 11:13).

So many of us are afraid to ask God for His help and accept His eternal salvation. My dad told me more than once, "If you were having a meal with me, would you be afraid to ask me to pass the salt?" Of course I would not be afraid to ask. I would say, "Please pass the salt," and my dad would pass it to me. Dad said, "Then if you are comfortable asking me to pass the salt to enhance your meal, do you not think that inviting God into your life would also be granted in the same way?"

Many of us have a difficult time asking for direction and help in prayer, and the same principle applies here. Matthew states, "Ask and it will be given to you; seek and you will find; knock and the door will be opened to you" (Matthew 7:7). There is a clear direction stated here. Knock on the door for eternity to be opened to you. Here is the deal: the day you accept Christ, you start your eternal journey. You will pass from this earthly world into a heavenly, eternal existence, living forever with Jesus.

Which would you choose? A life living with Jesus as your protector, Savior, and friend or a life of continued addiction, sorrow, and defeat? I know full well that a life void of Jesus is not the way I want to live ever again. I just wish I had known the better everlasting choice sooner, but I know now, and that is all that counts.

If you don't think you are good enough, that is BS. You are fearfully and wonderfully made. "I praise you because I am fearfully and wonderfully made; your works are wonderful, I know that full well" (Psalm 139:14). It is time for you to wake up and realize that this verse applies to you and your future. Or maybe you are reading this thinking of a person in your life who needs to be taken from the claws of addiction. It is time to act, to get help for you or the person you are thinking of at this moment. We are only a heartbeat away from eternity in heaven or hell. As a realtor will tell you, it is all about location, location, location.

Please don't take this juncture in your life, or the life of the person(s) you are thinking of at this moment, lightly. Reach out, seek Jesus, trust Jesus, live for Jesus, love Jesus. Tell the

Getting Help

person you are thinking of about Jesus. This might be the only chance you have to share the gift of eternity with them.

Your outlook and attitude on life will undergo a remarkable and lasting change that will amaze you. Struggles will be there, but you have the Creator and Warrior on your team who willingly gave His life for you, gave His life so you may live forever in His kingdom that He is preparing for you. "My Father's house has many rooms; if that were not so, would I have told you that I am going there to prepare a place for you?" (John 14:2).

Jesus came from heaven from the direction of His Father. He changed the world in three years and sacrificed His life on the cross so we may live. His life was without sin. Therefore, if Jesus said it, it is true: you can bet your eternal life on that. This is the moment you need to decide for you, for your friends. What will you choose? It's not up to me to make that choice for you. You are in the driver's seat. This is the time to make positive decisions for yourself. I know you can do that. Trust Jesus.

I accepted Christ late in my addicted adult life. My life did not reflect the life Jesus intended for me. But His protection was consistently there. Because of my lifestyle choice, I found myself in a pit of despair countless times. But Jesus continued to protect me. Because, yes, with Jesus, you can fix stupid. I did. That does not mean I will live a life without challenges, temptations, and trials. However, I have a Savior who gives me hope and an eternity with Him. I can go forward, looking toward a future of walking with God by my side.

I should be an ugly-looking drug hag. But I am not. I don't know why God spared my looks and my life. (I am thankful He did!) Yes, I have lost all my teeth and wear upper and lower dentures. Jesus loves me and I am a child of God. I praise Him every day for my life, my life now and my life then.

In Proverbs, there is this verse: "As iron sharpens iron, so one person sharpens another" (Proverbs 27:17). There will be sparks as the iron is sharpened. There was pruning from God as He was working with me. I had to hit bottom before I surrendered to His will. I believe, in a sense, all of us need to bottom out, then the Master can work with us. My dad has said time and time again that God will continue to prune you like a gardener prunes a bush because the gardener knows that pruning allows for healthy growth. Dad also said that I would probably get so pruned that my nickname would be "Stubby." He was right. I was pruned so that all the addictive, cancerous growth and lifestyle were taken away.

Here is an example I like to use. Have you ever watched a potter work with clay? The first step is to toss the clay on the rotating wheel. The clay is never centered on the wheel at the start. However, with gentle hands, the potter guides the clay to the center of the wheel, where the clay no longer resists the wheel or the potter's will. It is the same for us. We need to be centered in God's will. We need to be centered on Jesus, not resisting Him, getting into a position that allows Him to mold us into a human vessel following His direction and will. Then the molding process will begin.

Let's say a potter is making a clay jar. To do this, the potter (in our life, the Creator) uses their fingers to push down into the clay, to create the jar using their skill. In pottery, this is called piercing the heart of the clay, like Jesus will pierce your heart to mold you. As the wheel continues to spin, the potter works deeper and deeper into the clay. Forming the sides, the design takes shape. Keeping the clay moist is critical: that is the living water in a way. Until the vessel takes the exact shape intended by the potter, the potter continues to mold the clay. The clay (us) is formed to the potter's will. Finally, there is a vessel, not a lump of clay but an object that can be poured into and out of. Think of that pouring as your life. God pours into you, and you pour out to others so God can fill you again and again.

However, the creative transformation is not complete. When the clay dries, it will become weak because it has not been fully processed. We are not completely formed either until the impurities are cast out of our lives. With clay, it must be what potters call "bone dry" to move the jar on to the next step. If any moisture remains, it will turn to steam in the firing process. That expansion will crack the object and make it useless. When the firing process starts, the temperature inside the kiln will rise to 2,400 degrees Fahrenheit. There is one more step, the glaze firing. This firing will make the product stronger and waterproof. This final procedure allows the clay to become ceramic. A glaze or coating is formed, creating a durable product. We are the clay, and as Jesus takes on the firing and becomes, if you will, the ceramic, He makes a strong bond with us.

Now are we ready to be used? How will we be in His will and not in His way?

If you don't like the road you're walking,
start paving another one.
—Dolly Parton

May the grace of the Lord Jesus Christ, and the love of God,
and the fellowship of the Holy Spirit be with you all.
—2 Corinthians 13:14

A Drug User's Prayer

Note: We could not find who wrote this prayer, so the only thing we can do is give credit to an anonymous writer.

> Lord, can you help teach me a way
> To bear the marks I have made?
> The needle tracks from shooting up
> The scars from cutting
> The nose bleeds from snorting too much crack,
> How about the bruises on my back?
> The payment for all the crap I smoked.
> Lord, I know I done you wrong
> I know my life won't last that long
> With the damage done
> I turn to you for help, Dear Lord.
> As my breath grows shorter, and I am
> Weak at last, I wish I had done this
> Sooner, you could have helped me long ago.
> Now I lay at death's door, remembering
> All the pain and hurt I caused.
> I pray, dear Lord, for a chance, just one more.
> I promise to behave and to change my old ways.
> I promise, dear Lord, to tell others of the misery
> That has befallen me, and the misery that I have caused
> And the hope that lays in you, so please
> Dear Lord, hear this drug user's prayer.
> Amen.

My Name Is Meth

~~~

This was written by a young girl who was in jail for drug charges and was addicted to meth. She wrote this while in jail. As you will soon read, she fully grasped the horrors of the drug, as she tells in this simple yet profound poem. She was released from jail, but, true to her story, the drug owned her. They found her dead not long after, with the needle still in her arm.

This poem was given to Dr. Jack Perkins, who said, "I take no credit for her work, and always remember, DON'T DO DRUGS!!!"

I destroy homes; I tear families apart, take your children, and that's just the start.

I'm more costly than diamonds, more precious than gold.
The sorrow I bring is a sight to behold.
If you need me, remember I'm easily round,

I live all around you—in schools and in town I live
With the rich; I live with the poor; I live down the street, and maybe next door.
I'm made in a lab, but not like you think. I can be made under the kitchen sink.

In your child's closet, and even in the woods,

If this scares you to death, well, it certainly should. I have many names, but there's one you know best,
I'm sure you've heard of me. My name is crystal meth.
My power is awesome; try me you'll see, but if you do, you may never break free. Just try me once and I might let you go, but try me twice, and I'll own your soul.

When I possess you. You'll steal and you'll lie. You do what you have to—
just to get high.

The crimes you'll commit for my narcotic charms
will be worth the pleasure you'll feel in your arms, your lungs, your nose.

You'll lie to your mother; you'll steal from your dad, when you see their tears, you should feel sad.

But you'll forget your morals
and how you were raised,
be your conscience, teach you my ways.

I take kids from parents, and parents from kids. I turn people from God, and separate friends.
I'll take everything from you, your looks and your pride; I'll be with you always—right by your side.

You'll give up everything—your family, your home, your friends, your money, then you'll be alone. Take and take till you have nothing more to give. When I'm finished with you, you'll be lucky to live.

If you try me be warned—this is no game. If given the chance, I'll drive you insane. I'll ravish your body, I'll control your mind,

I'll own you completely,

Your soul will be mine.

The Author of Life

By Susan Rehberg

Jesus reached down from heaven
and gathered a lump of clay,
pressing here, smoothing there;
a ray of sunshine for the hair;
a rose petal for the cheeks;
a touch of stardust for the eyes;
a song of angels for the lips.
On the heart He wrote,
"Made for Me."
Filling the lungs with His breath,
He gave His life for that lump of clay,
creating a work of art
that is to bear His name.
Therefore, my child,
you belong to Him.
May no one change
what He has authored.
May no one remove His copyright.
for you are His workmanship,
you are His story
for the world to read.[6]

For we are God's handiwork,
created in Christ Jesus to do good works.
—Ephesians 2:10

Conclusion

Do you remember the first door you walked through? It seems our lives are comprised of door after door.

Here is what I mean. Doors lead us to places we have never been before. Some doors are positive, and others are negative.

Jesus said, "I am the gate [door]; whoever enters through me will be saved. They will come in and go out, and find pasture. The thief comes only to steal and kill and destroy; I have come that they may have life, and have it to the full" (John 10:9–10). Jesus is standing at the door to your heart. He is waiting for you to open your door and invite Him in.

How many doors have you passed through that were not the best for you? Personally, I wish many of the doors I willingly opened and passed through had been locked. I know I walked through the doors of alcohol, drugs, and immoral physical acts. The doors of theft were waiting for me to open and travel to the other, darker side. There were the doors of lying and cheating, and these negative openings were trapdoors I traversed and fell through, only to realize, once on the other side, that there was not a handle with which to reopen the door and redirect my course. Eventually, I found myself trapped in a pit of despair with little or no hope.

At my lowest point, God's gift of salvation became accessible when I genuinely invited Him into my heart. Before I was a "buffet Christian," a little here and a little there. Never the entire meal.

In my past, I walked willingly through the devil's doors of abortion, self-inflicted wounds (cutting), and all the above doors that I just mentioned. Never again, never. Today and every day forward, I am trying to walk through any door that is in the will of my Jesus. I am a new person in Christ, not that this walk with Jesus beside me will be easy. Jesus, my eternal companion, was willing to die on a cross—a death more horrible than we can imagine—so that I could be saved. You think that was easy?

He opened the door to eternity for me. Read that statement again. *He opened the door to eternity for me,* but also for you. Read this verse several times. Let the truth soak in. "Now to him who is able to do immeasurably more than all we ask or imagine, according to his power that is at work within us" (Ephesians 3:20). You can have this power too.

And here is an action verse: "Ask and it will be given to you; seek and you will find; knock and the door will be opened to you. For everyone who asks receives; the one who seeks finds; and to the one who knocks, the door will be opened" (Matthew 7:7–8).

How many doors have you gone through where there could have been a better choice? Isn't it time to enter eternity by opening the door to your heart and soul? We have all fallen short of the glory of God. "If you declare with your mouth, 'Jesus is Lord,' and believe in your heart that God raised him from the dead, you will be saved" (Romans 10:9).

Jesus's followers, we believers, will travel beyond their wildest imaginations. When Jesus conquered death, He earned the right to be *THE* door. Either you believe it or you don't. You can pass by the door or go through it.

Ask yourself this: where does Jesus want to take me? Am I willing to go? Am I willing to follow His will? Easter, when Jesus rose from the grave, is about life everlasting. You can rise

Conclusion

from your pit of despair; you can do more than you realize. Whatever addiction you have, there is a release. That release is the eternal power of Christ Jesus.

Can you put your feet to action and follow Him? Perhaps the pebble in your shoe will become your solid rock.

With love and prayer,
Jennifer

Acknowledgments

A big thank-you to all the beta and advanced copy readers (ARC) who dedicated their time to evaluate this project and give us valuable feedback. You know who you are, but the public doesn't. Thank you, beta readers: you carried a challenge and heavy burden. And to all the ARC readers, you are the most wonderful launch team an author could ask for. Jen and I opened our hearts, and you delicately held them in your loving hands.

And all of you who helped "jump start" this book financially. Without your support, this project would not have happened.

To Pastor Lee Eddy (friend, critic, author, continual student of the Word). To Jan Fallon (author), Susan Rehberg (poet of notes), Chaplain Doug Carver (Major General, retired), and John Weathers (high school friend). All of you helped hone this work. To Callie, my proofreader at www.proofcorrections.net: you are beyond the best. To my publisher, Michael Klassen, for many, many coffee sessions and phone calls of encouragement. You kept me on track when I wandered and wondered if I should even continue to write this book. Thanks to Jenn Clark for her continual direction on getting this book into the hands of you, the reader. To so many friends and prayer partners, who are not mentioned, the list is long. All of you held Jennifer and me up in prayer during those terribly addictive years, a deep thanks to you. Prayer works.

Acknowledgments

Finally, to Barbara, my wife, for your support and for listening to me fuss and fret about this book. You are a pillar of strength to me. (I know you are also a writer's widow more than you want to be.)

Finally, and most important, to my Lord and Savior, Jesus Christ: without Your unconditional love for all of us, this book would have not been possible. Through many prayers and because of Your thundering, silent urging, words were placed on paper.

Remember:

The author of your story still has the pen in His hand.
—John Boyer

Notes

[1] Kolmac, "Why Is Drug Abuse in America on the Rise?" July 10, 2020, https://www.kolmac.com/why-is-drug-use-in-america-on-the-rise/.

[2] Niki Monazzam and Kristen M. Budd, "Incarcerated Women and Girls," The Sentencing Project, March 2023, https://www.sentencingproject.org/app/uploads/2023/05/Incarcerated-Women-and-Girls-1.pdf

[3] Jeff Diamant, Besheer Mohamed, and Rebecca Leppert, "What the Data Says about Abortion in the U.S." Pew Research Center, March 25, 2024, https://www.pewresearch.org/short-reads/2024/03/25/what-the-data-says-about-abortion-in-the-us.

[4] WebMD, "Narcissism: Symptoms and Signs," March 30, 2023, https://www.webmd.com/mental-health/narcissism-symptoms-signs.

[5] Songwriters: Gloria Gaither / Willam J. Gaither, "Something Beautiful" lyrics, © BMG Rights Management, Capitol CMG Publishing, Sony/ATV Music Publishing LLC.

[6] Susan Rehberg, *A Time to Be Still* (Covington, Washington: EchoBay Publishing, 2004).

About the Authors

Robert N. Ruesch is a multi-published author with articles in magazines and local newspapers. He lives with his wife in the Denver, Colorado, area, enjoying every day that God gives him. When not writing, Robert likes working with other writers, helping them achieve their dreams.

Jennifer Lyn Ruesch (named after the Jenny biplane) is currently living with her father and bonus mom, as she continues to heal from the three decades plus of addiction and abuse that defined her life. Jennifer takes each day at a time, as God molds her into a directed and strong Christian woman. She has the goal of helping others who are in the clutches of addiction.

Both Robert and Jennifer are available to groups to share their story, the triumphs and the challenges, but more importantly, the protection of God and His redemptive powers.

Writing this book, with with each other, was a challenge, yet a true blessing. How do you tell the true story of a daughter's life of drugs, alcohol, deceit, and deep heartfelt sorrow? Between the pages, two lives converged, collided, separated, and came together with God's mercy and saving grace.

Printed in the USA
CPSIA information can be obtained
at www.ICGtesting.com
LVHW041039241124
797241LV00007B/727